THE
SHADY SIDE
OF AMERICA

★★★★★★★★★★★★★★★★★★★★★★★

THE
SHADY SIDE
OF AMERICA

★★★★★★★★★★★★★★★★★★★★★★★

A Roundup of the Scoundrels,
Deceivers, and Corrupters
Over 400-Odd Years Before Watergate

By George Bruce Woodin

with illustrations by
Charles E. Peterson and Audrey Wichern

BOLD FACE BOOKS, INC. NEW YORK
Distributed by
Sterling Publishing Co., Inc., New York

Other Books by George Bruce Woodin

A Fresh Look At American History (five volumes)
Popular Superstitions
All You Need to Know About Wine
All You Need to Know About Herbs & Spices

To Mary, my partner in life

© 1974 by George Bruce Woodin
Published by Bold Face Books, Inc.
Distributed by Sterling Publishing Co., Inc.
419 Park Avenue South, New York, N.Y., 10016
British edition published by Oak Tree Press Co., Ltd., Nassau, Bahamas
Distributed in Australia and New Zealand by Oak Tree Press Co., Ltd.,
P.O. Box J34, Brickfield Hill, Sydney 2000, N.S.W.
Distributed in the United Kingdom and elsewhere in the British Commonwealth
by Ward Lock Ltd., 116 Baker Street, London W 1
Manufactured in the United States of America
All rights reserved
Library of Congress Catalog Card No.: 74–82323
Sterling ISBN 0-8069–2018–1 Trade   Oak Tree 7061–2043–4
2019-X Library

CONTENTS

THE HISTORIAN should be fearless and incorruptible; a man of independence, loving frankness and truth; one who, as the poet says, calls a fig a fig and a spade a spade. He should yield to neither hatred nor affection, but should be unsparing and unpitying. He should be neither shy nor deprecating, but an impartial judge, giving each side all it deserves but no more. He should know in his writings no country and no city; he should bow to no authority and acknowledge no king. He should never consider what this or that man will think, but should state the facts as they really are.

LUCIAN: *How History Should Be Written*
Circa 170

PUBLISHER'S NOTE

As this book will show you, a natural alliance has existed between politicians, historians, and schoolteachers to keep from students, and the public in general, many of the incidents, facts, and attitudes of the leaders in American history. No doubt the same alliance exists abroad, and perhaps has existed throughout man's presence on earth, for it is only natural to remember and stress the good, to present the best face possible, and to hide the evil, especially the unsuccessful.

Without knowing all the facts, how can one make the judgments required of the honest citizen, the voter, the student? It is with this in mind that the author and publisher decided to expose those events which have remained hidden to a large extent from the reading public, even though some prominent historians, here and there, have taken note and recorded those events.

What is to be achieved by bringing the evils, corruption, immoralities, and unethical behavior of American leaders out into the open? For one thing, it may have the desirable effect of reducing hero worship to the point where victory on the battlefield, and "charisma," become unacceptable as reasons for election to office. America has built heroes out of men who are not perfect. This book shows that. But do we need perfection? Don't we need men who are human, torn by the same temptations and problems that "common people" have? Was Jefferson less of a leader because of his faults, or more of a leader because he personally practiced miscegenation and could understand the black people better, though he could not admit to it in public?

Second, the long history of corruption in America shows that the attainment of high office has always held an allure (sometimes financial) for the politician, the lawyer who specializes in lawmaking, and the party follower who hopes by devotion to reach high office. The Constitution never provided for political parties, but they sprang up through man's natural desire to divide the masses into "ins" and "outs." What America has done with the two-party system shows up here strong and clear, to be examined and considered seriously.

Third comes justice—and injustice. Our system makes an attempt to distinguish between the two, but the line between is thin. Much injustice has been practiced in the name of justice, not only by the courts but by men of good repute.

Fourth, this book shows that men do change, though not necessarily for the better, and that there is hope for further change. Because our present government has evolved from a base that is strong in principle, and weak (often corrupt) in practice, is no excuse for the current deceptions of the public. The magnitude of corruption and deceit has never been so great as it is today. This study of the "shady side" enables us to see step-by-step how we reached the point where a President can lie almost all of the time and still seem credible to a majority of the people, while not fooling the newspapermen at all. The public believe the man they elect President, and tend to disbelieve the lowly reporter. (Just as some people will tend to disbelieve the author of this book, although he has himself substantiated and given authorities in the Notes and Sources for every statement he makes.)

The publisher believes that this book will become as valuable to the student of history as others of its kind, and that it will lead to a new type of history textbook, one which reveals everything and does not sweep under the carpet those facts that politicians would rather hide.

It is far more patriotic to be proud of your country, despite its faults and mistakes, than to wave a flag in an effort to hide them.

I
THE EARLY EXPLORERS

WAS COLUMBUS JEWISH?

America was discovered quite accidentally by a great seaman whose name was said to be Cristóbal Colón rather than Christopher Columbus, and whose family background was said to be Spanish and Jewish rather than Italian and Catholic.

If this was true, Columbus himself must have been struck by the irony of the situation; for he began his diary of the "great adventure," writing: "After the Spanish monarchs [King Ferdinand and Queen Isabella] had expelled all the Jews from their kingdoms and lands . . . they commissioned me to undertake the voyage . . . with a properly equipped fleet."

Hopeful of finding an ocean route to the Orient, Columbus left Palos on August 3, 1492, the day after the last Jew was supposed to be out of anti-Semitic Spain. Five men who manned his ships were Jews. One of them, Rodrigo de Triana, was the first to sight land in the New World; another held the important post of fleet physician. Four of Columbus's principal supporters —Diego de Deza, Juan Cabrero, Gabriel Sanchez, and Alfonso de la Caballeria—were Jews, as were Abraham Senior and Isaac Abravanel, who supplied his ships,

11

and Abraham Zacuto, who drew up the navigation charts for his voyage. And why did Columbus send the first news of his success to Luis de Santangel, a Jewish friend and the manager of the royal household, rather than to the king and queen?

Good at seamanship but poor at geography, Columbus mistook the West Indies for the East Indies and thought that the Arawak Indians were Orientals. His sailors, having spent more than two months at sea, quickly took up with the native girls and gave them two of civilization's most popular diseases: gonorrhea and syphilis.

WERE THE INDIANS JEWS?

Some 150 years after Columbus's discovery, an English theologian, the Reverend Thomas Thorowgood, authored a book—*Jews in America, or Probabilities That the Americans Are of That Race*—in which he contended that the American Indians, whose religious rites were reportedly similar to those of the Jews, were actually descendants of the ancient Israelites. Later, William Penn, the founder of Pennsylvania, advanced the same argument, claiming that the American aborigines bore certain physical resemblances to the Jews he remembered seeing in the ghetto of his native London.

AMERICA WRONGLY NAMED

By a strange comedy of errors, the New World was named after Amerigo Vespucci, an Italian who turned Spanish, and who never commanded a voyage of discovery in his life. He did make three or four trips to South America, but only as a passenger and junior officer. There were letters, written and published by Vespucci, about these "South American cruises," but, except for some spicy items about the sex life of the Indians, they might have been written about someone else's trips. The credit that Vespucci got for having discovered a new continent was due largely to the work of a young German teacher named Martin Waldseemuller, who was "sold" enough on the "great explorer" to write in his *Cosmographiae Introductio:* "Since Amerigo Vespucci has discovered a fourth part of the world, it should be called after him . . . America, since Europe and Asia got their names from women." The idea spread, and by 1530, almost everyone in Europe was calling the New World AMERICA. Columbus, unsung and neglected by the royal court, yet managed to make a statement for the record before his death in 1506: "By the Divine Will I have placed under the sovereignty of the King and Queen an Other World, whereby Spain . . . is to become the richest of all countries."

SPANISH CRUELTIES

King Ferdinand and Queen Isabella thought that the Indians should be "treated kindly and quickly converted to Christianity." But something went wrong, and they were soon treated more like animals than human beings. Hungry for gold, the Spaniards wasted no time in putting the Indians to work until death in the mines, while their missionaries were introducing the idea of the crucifixion—a torture which the Indians soon adopted for enemies they could not forgive. In no time, the innocence of the New World became nothing more than a bedtime story.

The Spanish explorers, who followed in the wake of Columbus, spent the next 50 years (1492–1542) trying to go through or around America to get their greedy hands on the riches of China, India, and Japan. As described by historians, they must have devoted as much of their time to drinking, raping, and murdering as they did to grabbing land from the Indians, in the name of God and King.

INDIANS CRUCIFIED:
Spanish missionaries gave
natives of the New World
the choice of accepting
Christianity or facing death.

Hernando Cortés, expecting to find a "mountain of solid gold," landed on the coast of Mexico, and, by cutting off the water supply, conquered the wealthy empire of the Aztec Indians and their great leader, Montezuma, who was later brutally put to death by a Spanish swordsman. The taking of the plains of Teotihuacan completed the ruin of Aztec power and enabled Spain to claim Mexico as her own.

Francisco Pizarro, commanding a fleet of ships built in Panama, invaded Peru in 1531 and treacherously seized and murdered Atahualpa, the friendly emperor of the Inca Indians, who had welcomed him. The natives, lacking a leader, still fought bravely for six years before they finally gave up their land.

The Spaniards acquired more territory in the New World in one generation than the Romans conquered in the Old World in 500 years. But, after 1588, when Spain became weaker and other seafaring nations became stronger, other explorers carried the flags of England, France, and the Netherlands to America, bringing with them a new bag of dirty tricks, including the practice of scalping.

THE DUTCH BRING LIQUOR

Henry Hudson, an Englishman working for the Dutch, sailed up the Hudson River in 1609 and made the big mistake of offering hard liquor to the Mohawks in exchange for furs. Other Indians, learning that drinking and trading could be pleasurable as well as profitable, took to the bottle with disastrous results.

The Dutch West India Company, plying the Manhattan Indians with Holland gin, made the "greatest real estate bargain in history." The Indians, high as kites, gave up the island bearing their name for a pile of trinkets worth no more than $24. But New Amsterdam, as New York City was then called, turned out to be a total failure as a Dutch colony. The various governors, described by writer Washington Irving as "figures of fun," were actually petty autocrats who ruled with an iron hand, used torture to get confessions out of lawbreakers, and mismanaged everything, including the Indians. One of them, a peglegged soldier named Peter

WHITES CHEATED
INDIANS out of valuable
furs and real estate, by
getting them drunk on hard
liquor.

Stuyvesant, surrendered the entire island to British attackers in 1664, without firing a shot.

THE FRENCH PLANT THEIR FLAG

Jacques Cartier, who got France interested in Canada, made two voyages to America in the years 1533–35, sailing up and down the river, which he named the St. Lawrence. The Huron Indians, taking to the friendly Frenchman, entertained him nightly with tall stories of a "Kingdom of Saguenay," inhabited by white men who ran gold, silver, and diamond mines, flew like bats, and never ate. Cartier not only bought the whole package, but also got the Huron chief to accompany him to France and sell it to the king, which he did. "Canadian diamonds" became the joke of the day in Paris.

Samuel Champlain, described as the "father of New France," broke up a friendship between the Huron and Iroquois Indians, and, by encouraging them to fight among themselves, managed to get his hands on a choice piece of Canadian real estate, and to have a lake named after him. The French flag still flies in gay Quebec.

VIRGINIA GOES TOBACCO MAD

England, seeing the advantages of exploring and grabbing land in the New World, put much of her faith in Captain John Smith, who crossed the Atlantic in 1607, to set up a colony at Jamestown, Virginia. The legend of Pocahontas as the savior of the gallant captain's life from her Indian tribe was probably invented by the Englishman; the Indian princess herself, later glorified as dignified and innocent, was described by John Rolfe, her English husband, as "one whose education hath been rude, her manners barbarous, her generation accursed."

The colony, which was made up largely of Londoners who had left their homeland to get out of paying their bills, suffered from hard times, but saved itself by growing the "weed." America went "tobacco mad," and, as the years passed, the Randolphs, Dukes, and other "First Families of Virginia" made millions promoting the "dirty habit."

With all of this going on, many Europeans looked upon the New World as a "sad disappointment."

2
IMPURE PURITANS

THE PURITANS BREAK THEIR WORD

The Pilgrims and the Puritans, fed up with the rigors of
Catholicism and the way in which King James I was
mixing religion with politics, left England aboard the
Mayflower in the autumn of 1620. Arriving at Plymouth,
Massachusetts, 64 days later, they made plans for a
colony and drew up an agreement, promising that there
would be religious and political freedom, and "just and
equal laws" for all comers. But these promises, all voiced
solemnly by John Winthrop, William Bradford, and
other leaders of the expedition, were as readily broken as
pie crusts.

Within a short time, they forgot most of the high
principles that they had talked about and refused to give
others the same sort of treatment that they wanted for
themselves. Only Puritans were allowed to run the
Massachusetts government, and only church members
in good standing were allowed to vote and hold public
office. Anyone who made so bold as to criticize what the
church or government was doing was given a quick trial
and a jail sentence. And to make certain that everyone
went to church on Sunday, the moral policemen of the
parish got a law passed so that absentees would have to
pay heavy fines.

PURITAN SIN

Above all else, the Puritans wanted to establish a community rather than a mere colony, where they could put their "ideals" into practice. New England, to them, was a New Canaan which the Almighty had set apart for an experiment in Christian living. They felt, as Winthrop had remarked when they landed at Plymouth, that they were a "city upon a hill," with "the eyes of all people upon them—an example to prove that it was possible to lead the New Testament life, and still make a living." As writer Gertrude Stein once put it when writing about the "purity" of the Puritans and their plans for a "godly life": "In New England they have done it they do do it they will do it and they do it in every way in which . . . it can be thought about."

It was no accident that almost every reformer and educational leader in American history has been a New Englander with a Puritan background. Puritanism, a rather dull way of life, put as much emphasis on the importance of work as it did on religion. The Reverend Hugh Peter of Salem, Massachusetts, announced in one of his Sunday sermons that "an hour's idleness is as bad as an hour's drunkenness."

PURITAN LAWBREAKERS WERE LET OFF EASY, with short sentences and light punishments, due to a shortage of jails and labor.

But try as they did to keep down sin and crime, the churchmen and lawmakers could not make all of the New Englanders follow the straight and narrow. Many a man and many a woman saw fit to use all of the four-letter words, play cards and throw dice, get drunk on hard cider or home-brewed beer, and do a bit of whoring. Five-month babies were not uncommon, and, in some cases, the adulterers were made to wear a scarlet letter "A" in public, an idea which first inspired Nathaniel Hawthorne's famous story, and later, an unforgettable movie, *The Scarlet Letter*.

HARVARD'S "HIPPIES"

Harvard College students, the "beatniks" of the day, wore their hair down to their shoulders, dressed up in crazy clothes, drank rum, and got themselves condemned by the clergy, who saw them as "sinners in need of divine punishment." The lawbreakers were usually given short sentences or light punishments, partly because there was a shortage of jails, and mostly because there was a shortage of labor.

THE PURITANS HUNT WITCHES

The Reverend Cotton Mather, the boy wonder of the New England clergy and the first person on record to use the word *American*, wrote a "how-to-do-it" book on witchcraft in 1692, telling how individuals "possessed by the devil" could be spotted and brought to trial. The book became a "best seller," and, within a short time, five men and 14 women were tried and sentenced to death by Chief Justice William Stoughton's witch court in Salem, Massachusetts. One man, Giles Corey, suffered the same fate, for scornfully refusing to plead guilty or not guilty. At least four others died in jail of the fever that swept through it; one poor child, jailed with her mother who was hanged, lost her mind. Some

50 "suspects" saved their skins by pleading guilty and accusing others. The near-madness did not end until 1693, when the witch hunters began to go after prominent people such as the Boston clergy and wealthy merchants.

INDIANS FORCED INTO SLAVERY

The Algonquin Indians of New England wanted many things that the English had to offer, such as firearms and tools, but the Puritans insisted on selling them "civilization" in a single package, Congregational church and all. The chiefs of the Wampanoags, Nipmucks, and Narragansetts refused to buy the idea, contending that they were not the least bit happy over the white man's grabbing their lands, breaking promises, and getting their warriors drunk. The Wampanoag tribe, which had kept the Pilgrims alive with food during their first winter in the New World, soon had their fill of bad treatment from the colonists, and decided that there was no way out except to go to war.

King Philip's War, as it was named after the chief of the Wampanoags, lasted from the spring of 1675 to the spring of 1676, and featured one of the fiercest battles ever fought on New England soil. The English, helped by "converted" Indians, won and forced the Wampanoags and their allies to move to the northern wilderness and other parts of the country. The warriors whom the English captured were sold as slaves in the West Indies, their squaws and children parceled out as servants to white families.

BLACKS FOR SALE

Although black slaves were not nearly as popular in New England as they were in other American colonies— particularly those in the South—they were still bought and sold in sizable numbers by the Puritans. New

England ship captains, sailing along the West African coast before heading for the Caribbean, picked up boatloads of blacks, whom they traded for molasses and rum. Pleased over the profits that Massachusetts was making in the slave trade, Governor John Winthrop neatly summed up his feelings by saying "it pleased the Lord to open us a trade . . . in the West Indies."

SMUGGLING STARTS

By the 1760's, some 90 per cent of the Puritans were members of the Congregational church. Social life centered in the "parish," and colonial governments— allowing *almost* every white adult male to vote—gave the people a chance to have their say. There were plenty of comfortable brick and wooden houses, built in the Georgian style, with beautiful interiors and well-kept gardens. The ship-owning merchants, who owned most of them, ranked socially with clergymen, lawyers, and physicians. Although there were no "modern amusements," there were still plenty of clean woods and streams for hunting and fishing, except on the Sabbath Day.

The seaports, not safe to walk in at night, were filled with a rough working class, consisting of sailors, shipbuilders, and rowdies, who were ever willing to listen to agitators and rabble-rousers. King George III had good reason to worry about them. For they were not only smuggling goods to get out of paying import duties, but were also listening to militants like Samuel Adams, who wanted to rebel against the British Crown.

All things considered, the Pilgrims and the Puritans may have fallen short in planting the seed of religious and political freedom—and in establishing a "godly way of life"—but they certainly laid, without knowing it, the "egg" of democracy.

3
BLACKS WITHOUT RIGHTS

The first Afro-Americans, leaving Africa aboard a Dutch ship for America in 1619, landed at Jamestown, Virginia, and, like many of the poor whites who came from Europe, were "indentured servants," not slaves. That is, they served their employers, without pay, for a period of, say, three to 10 years to reimburse them for what they had paid out for the trip across the Atlantic. But, within a short time, the blacks were treated altogether differently from the whites. The whites, completing their agreed-upon working period, were set free and allowed to do as they pleased; the blacks, on the other hand, were in most cases made to work for the rest of their lives. Increasingly, the whites became more clearly *free*; the blacks, more clearly *slave*.

SLAVERY MADE LEGAL

The same Englishmen who had left England because they did not like her laws, now drew up a bit of legislation that would have been frowned upon by the courts of England: a so-called black code. From 1660 on, the English in America could legally own slaves,

BLACKS WERE BOUGHT AND SOLD like cattle and horses, and often treated badly by slaveholders in the 1600's.

but the English in England could not. The promise of freedom in America that the Pilgrims and the Puritans had talked so much about was for whites only, and not for people of a different color.

Within a short space of time, almost every American city had a slave market, where blacks were bought and sold like cattle and horses. The father of a black family would often be sold to one slaveholder, his wife to another, and his children to still another. Black families seldom grew up together, and black children seldom knew their fathers.

MISCEGENATION

Although miscegenation (interracial sex) was made illegal by many of the colonial governments, and considered immoral by the churches, many white men— some as historically famous as Thomas Jefferson—slept with their slaves. As was reported by James T. Callendar in the *Richmond Recorder* in 1802, "it was well known that Jefferson kept Sally Hemings, one of his slaves, as a concubine and had fathered children by her." The features of Tom, the eldest offspring, were said "to bear a striking although sable resemblance to the statesman."

Supporting Callendar's charge was the fact that the entire Hemings family got special treatment from Jefferson. Sally's five children were all well taken care of by him. Sally herself was given a trip to Paris. All of the slaves freed by Jefferson were Hemingses, and none of Sally's children were retained in slavery as adults.

White women, too, had their "moments" with the

JEFFERSON'S SLAVE SON grew up to resemble him. If Jefferson had freed his slave-mistress, Sally Hemings, she would have had to leave Virginia with her five Jeffersonian children. Actually, Sally and her family were set free under Jefferson's will.

"blackamoors." James Bowdoin, a prominent Boston merchant, had to ship one of his slaves back to the West Indies, explaining that the fellow "had become too involved with some of the white women of the town." As pointed out by Anne Grant in *Memoirs of an American Lady; With Sketches of Manners and Scenes in America As They Existed Previous to the Revolution*, many a white woman in New England gave birth to a "dark-skinned child."

FRANKLIN ANTI-BLACK

Benjamin Franklin, believing that America should belong to "white people," wrote: "I could wish their Numbers were increased. And while we are, as I may call it, *Scouring* our Planet, by clearing America of Woods, and so making this Side of our Globe reflect a brighter Light to the Eyes of Inhabitants in Mars or Venus, why should we in the Sight of Superior Beings, darken its People? Why increase the Sons of Africa, by Planting them in America, where we have so fair an Opportunity, by excluding all Blacks and Tawneys, of increasing the lovely White and Red? But perhaps I am partial to the Complexion of my Country . . . for such Partiality is natural to Mankind."

With all of his fancy language, Franklin was expressing an important feeling, one which a famous Virginian, William Byrd, summed up more directly: "They import so many Negroes hither, that I fear this Colony will some time or other be confirmed by the Name of New Guinea."

In 1775, when the American Revolution broke out, there were almost as many slaves in the North as there were in the South. Blacks in New York were no better off than those in Virginia. Here and there, some people, such as the Quakers, spoke out against slavery. The Reverend Samuel Hopkins of Newport, Rhode Island (a colony founded by Roger Williams, a "left-wing Puritan," who believed in "freedom for all"), asked why Americans saw blacks as "fit for nothing but slavery." But few people listened to what the antislavers had to say. The captains of slave ships, sailing to and from Africa, continued to buy or to take blacks by force from their tribes.

SLAVES FOR THE FOUNDING FATHERS

Many Americans (James Madison, James Monroe, Edmund Randolph, et al), whose family names became famous in history books, either bought or sold slaves for profit, or used them as servants and laborers.

George Washington kept some 200 slaves busy from dawn to dusk on his Virginia tobacco plantation. As commander-in-chief of the Continental Army (as the Army of the United Colonies was often called, even to 1783), he twice turned down the idea of accepting blacks, and gave an order in 1775 forbidding recruiting officers to enlist "Negroes, boys unable to bear arms, and old men. . . ." But as things turned out, the racial policy of both the Army and Navy in the American Revolution was, in the end, largely determined by what the British did.

John Murray Dunmore, the royal governor of Virginia, promised freedom to all blacks who were willing to run away from their masters and bear arms for King George III. The Virginia slaveholders became alarmed over the prospect of losing their slaves, and General Washington became alarmed over the prospect of growing British strength. The general, supported by the Continental Congress, changed his mind about black enlistees. By the end of the war, some five thousand blacks had fought and won their freedom. But, as time marched on, it became all too clear to Paul Cuffe and other black leaders that the benefits gained from the war were for whites, not blacks.

4
FRANCE IN AMERICA

New France, now called Canada, was originally owned by a large French fur-trading company, known as The Hundred Associates. The company, established in 1627 by Samuel Champlain and Cardinal Richelieu (the power behind the French throne), gladly welcomed Catholic missionaries, farmers, and fur trappers, but wanted no other people on its property, especially if they were non-Catholic. As Count Frontenac, one of the early French governors, once remarked: "There are but two kinds of business in New France—the conversion of souls and the conversion of beaver." In 1665, Quebec had only 70 houses and 550 people, and one quarter of the population was made up of priests.

BEAVERS AND BRANDY

The fur trappers, traveling deeply into the woods, spent the winter trading and cheating the Indians, and collecting large quantities of furs. Came spring, they took to canoes and made their way down the St. Lawrence River to Montreal, where beaver pelts were worth a gold dollar each. In a good season a "runner of the woods" could make upward to $600, a lot of money in those days.

The fur buyers, lined up along the docks of the city, offered the trappers plenty of entertainment, including hard liquor, gambling, and girls. Booths were set up with all sorts of merchandise for sale; bars dispensed well-watered French brandy, a quart of which bought a beaver pelt; and there were gaming tables, where a trapper could gamble away every fur that he owned on a few throws of the dice.

The governor usually showed up to give a "loyalty speech" to the visiting Indians, while priests tried to preach religion to the merrymaking Frenchmen. But after a day or two of doing business, the trappers got so involved with drinking, gambling, and whoring that the governor and the good fathers had no choice but to leave.

PRIESTS EXPLORING

The priests and the fur trappers were often used as "tools" for French expansion. Father Jacques Marquette and Louis Joliet were the first Europeans to float down the Mississippi River. And eventually, after Robert de la Salle had explored the river, the French established New

PRIESTS TRIED TO SAVE SOULS, but French fur traders preferred wine, women, and song, to sermons, psalms and hymns.

Orleans in 1718, thereby dominating the mouth of the Mississippi and completing the grand design that they had in mind for controlling the American West.

Louis XIV, the French king, had hoped that New France would become a farming country, where citizens would be made to behave themselves, and where they would be told how to think by parish priests. As historians related it, one of the main reasons why young fur trappers took to the woods so readily was to get away from the "snooping church." The clergy in French Canada employed the most effective system of thought control ever to be used in America, north of Mexico. They made certain, too, that no "unapproved" book ever got to Canada.

The Canadians caused quite an uproar in Massachusetts in the late 1600's, when they sent fur trappers and priests to Maine to do business with the Abnaki Indians, and to convert them to the Catholic faith. The Reverend Cotton Mather, who was then preaching to English Puritans in Boston, rose to say, "We shall never be at rest till we have Canada."

The destruction of Canada as a French colony became one of the most important objectives of the New Englanders, for nearly 70 years. No small wonder, then, that the Canadians often spoke of the English colonies as "the bastards," or that French kings looked forward to the destruction of Boston.

GIRLS IMPORTED

The Hundred Associates, unable to get along with the Iroquois Indians, gave up Canada in 1663 and handed her over to Louis XIV. The king took over quickly, and Canada became a royal French colony. The Marquis de Tracy, Canada's first military governor, brought close to a thousand troops from France, who were given both land and wives.

FREE LOVE WAS POPULAR:
Indian girls, unlike French maidens, did not insist on marriage before sex.

No fewer than nine hundred girls were imported in the next 10 years. Upon arrival in Quebec, they were immediately sorted into three groups—good-family girls, middle-class-family girls, and poor-family girls. The fattest of the lot, viewed as the best workers and bedwarmers, were snapped up first. Dowries were provided by the generous king, and every girl found a husband within two weeks of her arrival. But the fur trappers, liking "local talent," often preferred Indian girls, because they did not insist on marriage.

By 1672, there were about eight thousand French settlers in Canada, most of whom lived along the banks of the St. Lawrence River. The government had wanted to stretch settlement farther westward, but Bishop Laval and the priests were afraid that the fur trappers, growing in number, might corrupt the Indians with booze and sex.

5
REBELLION IN VIRGINIA

POOR WHITES AND INDIANS

Virginia, faced with problems involving poor whites and Indians, came close to having an all-out war in 1675–76.

The poor whites, mostly servants, laborers, and tenant farmers, had grown tired of paying heavy taxes, while the wealthy plantation owners and politicians were paying little or nothing. After 1670, only landowners had a right to vote or to take part in political affairs. The children of landless men, with no schools to go to, had no chance for an education. Only the rich and powerful held public office, and most of them hired private teachers to instruct their children in reading, writing, and arithmetic. What the poor people needed most was a spokesman who would see to it that they got a fair deal.

Meanwhile, the Susquehannock Indians, who were even worse off than the poor whites when it came to having any rights, had grown tired of the way in which settlers were grabbing their hunting grounds. In August, 1675, three of the land-grabbers got into a heated argument with the Indians and wound up getting themselves killed. The militiamen of both

WASHINGTON AND TRUMAN SLAUGHTERED SUSQUEHAN-NOCKS: The Indians were put to death when they protested against whites grabbing their lands.

Virginia and Maryland were called out; Virginia's were led by Colonel John Washington, one of George's ancestors; Maryland's, by Major John Truman, who was not related in any way to Harry S.

The Susquehannocks sent out five chiefs to talk things over with Washington and Truman, but instead of listening to them, the officers had the tribal chieftains taken away and put to death. From that day on, if a Virginian or a Marylander could not find the right Indian to punish for some wrongdoing, he killed the first one that he met; a Susquehannock, in turn, felt that he had the right to kill any paleface that he met.

Worried about Indians on the warpath, the land-grabbers went to Governor William Berkeley of Virginia to ask him for protection. But the governor gave them nothing but promises. Indian haters, anxious for the blood of the Susquehannocks, spread the word around that "Berkeley doth not take a speedy course and destroy the redskins, owing to his wanting to trade with them."

The people who felt this way soon found a leader in Nathaniel Bacon, whom historians have variously described as the "torchbearer of democracy" and a "desperate rabble-rouser."

Bacon, who had been thrown out of Cambridge University for his "extravagancies," was the owner of two large tobacco plantations, and a member of the Virginia Assembly. A clever politician, he was on his way to becoming a member of the "ruling class," when one of his plantation supervisors got killed in a Susquehannock raid. Bacon's anger rose, and when he appeared before a group of local militiamen and gave vent to his feelings, he was greeted with cries of, "A Bacon, a Bacon!" This went to the fellow's head. Asked to become their commander, "General" Bacon led the Virginians in a fight against the Indians. But, instead of going after the guilty Susquehannocks, he attacked the innocent Occaneechees, accused them of sheltering the enemy, and brutally killed Persicles, their chief.

Besides this boo-boo, there was also a bit of interracial sex that caused General Bacon some embarrassment. As reported by Winthrop D. Jordan in *White Over Black*, Richard Lawrence, one of the general's top lieutenants, had made the big mistake of being caught "in the darke imbraces of a Blackamoor, his slave: And that in so fond a Maner . . . to the no meane Scandle . . . about towne." Learning about this, the militiamen refused to take any orders from Lawrence. To save face, Bacon fired him on the spot.

But, in spite of everything that had taken place, Bacon remained a hero and was picked as the spokesman of the people and the leader of the rebellion. Puffed up by the praises of his followers, he hastened to take his seat in the Assembly at Williamsburg, where, much to his surprise, he was seized by Governor Berkeley, who had become furious over his actions.

Luck was on Bacon's side. A messenger, covered with dirt and mud from a rough horseback ride, rushed into the Assembly to bring news of an Indian uprising at the

VIRGINIANS REBELLED: Settlers were against their government, and anxious for the blood of Indians.

upper reaches of the James and York Rivers—and, in the confusion that followed, Bacon ran out the door. But, within an hour's time, he returned, leading some 400 militiamen. The governor, madder than ever, faced up to him, shouting, "Here! Shoot me! 'Fore God, a fair mark my chest makes, shoot!"

Bacon, keeping his "cool," answered softly, "No, may it please your honor, we will not hurt a hair of your head, nor any man's. We are come for a commission to save our lives from the Indians, which you have so often promised, and now we will have it before we go."

His militiamen, shaking their cocked rifles at the windows of the Assembly, shouted in chorus, "We will have it! We will have it!"

Addressing the entire Assembly in strong words for close to one hour, Bacon demanded protection for the settlers, an auditing of the colony's books, the establishment of schools, a reduction of taxes, and other reforms.

Governor Berkeley, wanting peace and quiet more than anything else, added to his past promises, and then called in 1,200 Gloucester and Middlesex militiamen, ordering them to put down the rebel Bacon. But the men simply turned their backs and marched away, mumbling, "Bacon, Bacon, Bacon . . ."

Open warfare followed, and General Bacon became the master of all of Virginia except for the Eastern Shore. But he had no chance to win in the end. On sober second thought, many of the very men who had bawled, "A Bacon, a Bacon!" wilted at the thought of opposing the royal governor, and deserted.

At Yorktown, where Bacon made his last try for victory, he came down with a bad case of the "bloody flux" (dysentery), and there he died on October 26, 1676.

6
PIRACY IN
THE WEST INDIES

Within the short space of 50 years (1625–75), England, France, and the Netherlands set up a number of colonies in the West Indies, the most popular of which were Barbados, Jamaica, the Bahamas, Aruba and Curaçao. Spain, whose claims to Caribbean real estate had been well established by Christopher Columbus, decided to concentrate on Cuba, Puerto Rico, Trinidad, and other larger territories, which seemed to offer greater riches. The Carib Indians, well remembering the missionaries who had given their families the choice of accepting Christianity or being burned at the stake, did everything possible to keep Europeans off their property. But, within a few years, the Indians lost all of it to the land-grabbing invaders.

RUM, SLAVES, AND MISTRESSES

Barbados, the wealthiest of the English colonies, had some 23,000 whites and about 20,000 blacks in 1660. Life, which centered largely around the use of slave labor in the growing of sugar and the making of rum, was both rough and riotous. Sober London merchants who visited the island at about this time were shocked by the atmosphere of brutality and drunkenness. Commenting

CARIB INDIANS WERE
BURNED TO DEATH
when they tried to keep
whites from taking their real
estate.

on the rum business, one of them wrote: "The chief fudling [intoxicating liquor] they make in the Island is Rumbullion, alias Kill-Devill, which is a hott, hellish, and terrible liquor . . . made of distilled sugar canes."

As described by Bryan Edwards in his *History of the British West Indies*, the white men of Barbados, like those of the other Caribbean islands, thought nothing of sleeping with black women and did not care whether their white wives knew about it or not. The black slaves, subjected to severe cruelties by their white masters, often got their initials burned on their backs so that they could be readily identified.

PIRATES AND REBELS

Before the English could call Jamaica their own, they had to fight a short war with the Dutch, who were then the allies of France and Spain. Henry Morgan, the "prince of pirates," made good use of the island as a headquarters and hid much of his stolen treasure there. Grabbing Spanish ships which were loaded with gold and silver taken from the Indians in Central and South America, he became the richest man in the West Indies. In 1668, King Charles II of England showed his gratitude for the "cut" that he got from Captain Henry Morgan by making him Sir Henry Morgan.

The Bahamas, which boasted the largest pirate population in the West Indies, was largely run by Edward Teach, better known as "Blackbeard." Englishmen outside the "profession" stayed clear of places like Nassau until 1787, when King George III ousted the buccaneers and established law and order.

Philippe de Poincy, who managed Martinique, Guadeloupe, Saint-Domingue, and other Caribbean islands for France, lived in a huge mansion with one hundred white servants and black slaves, whom he treated badly. His "chief pirate," Pierre D'Esnambuc, killed all of the Carib Indians on St. Christopher (St. Kitts), and then divided the 23-mile-long island with Thomas Warner, an Englishman, who had helped him with the scalping of the natives.

The black slaves who were unlucky enough to be kept in Saint-Domingue finally rebelled toward the end of the 1700's and succeeded not only in freeing themselves, but also in setting up the second independent nation in the New World, which they renamed Haiti. Much to the surprise of their leader, Toussaint L'Ouverture,

WHITES BRANDED BLACKS used as slaves so that they could always be easily identified.

America, which had only recently won her independence from Great Britain, offered to trade with the new nation, *but* withheld diplomatic recognition. Only a handful of American antislavers had spoken out in favor of the rebellion, and none of the leading American newspapers supported it. Senator Joseph Clay of Pennsylvania described it as "black despotism and usurpation."

MONEYMAKING DUTCHMEN

The Dutch, by no means idle in the West Indies in the 17th century, did fairly well for themselves. Their favorite sea dog, Admiral Piet Hein, got away with a bit of piracy that every buccaneer had dreamed about for 50 years—the capturing of a fleet of eight Spanish treasure ships, en route from Latin America to Barcelona, with cargoes of coffee, cotton, ginger, indigo for making blue dye, and silver. The lot netted nearly $10 million to the Dutch West India Company, which had put up the money for the admiral's adventure.

When they were able to make piracy profits such as this, the Dutch paid little attention to real estate, no matter whether it was in the West Indies or along the banks of the Delaware and Hudson Rivers. They did decide, however, to take over a few Caribbean islands before the English and French grabbed them all. About 1630, the flag of the Netherlands went up over St. Martin's, where the Dutchmen beat down the Carib Indians and set up a plant to take salt from sea water. They also took Aruba and Curaçao, which became famous for an orange liqueur.

The English and French, who did much better at keeping the real estate that they had grabbed than the Spanish and Dutch did, became bitter rivals in the New World and fought each other over it for nearly one hundred years.

7
STUBBORN NEW ENGLAND

DID ENGLISH LAWS APPLY?

In 1677, when the New Englanders had just about finished off the Wampanoag Indians in King Philip's War, Charles II, the king of England, decided that it was high time the American colonists were made to obey the Crown's commercial laws, which they had long overlooked. After all, they were still Britishers, and why should they not be made to live by the laws of Britain? A reasonable bit of thinking on the king's part, but the people of Massachusetts refused to go along with it. Independent they were, and independent they would continue to be.

The Reverend Increase Mather, father of the famous Reverend Cotton Mather, suggested that the colonists try to "soften" the king with one of New England's favorite gift packages for very important people; namely, "ten barrells of cranberries, two hogsheads of special good samp [ground corn], and three thousand of cod fish." These items, which were hardly considered fit for the merry monarch's mouth, caused an uproar when they arrived at the royal palace in London. The king, whose stomach fairly turned upside down at the

NEW ENGLANDERS GOT NOWHERE with King Charles II when they tried to "soften" him with a gift package of American goodies.

thought of such rude food, became angrier than ever over his disobedient subjects and insisted that they be brought into line.

The colonists, helped by the Reverend Mather, drew up a bold reply to the royal command: "Wee humbly conceive," they said, "that the lawes of England are bounded within the four seas, and doe not reach America. The subjects of His Majesty here being not represented in Parliament, so we have not looked at ourselves to be impeded in our trade by them."

SMUGGLERS ON THE LOOSE

The king chose to pay no attention to this challenge. And for several years, he did nothing about the "stubborn New Englanders" except to send a tax collector named Edward Randolph, who got nowhere. The illegal traders and smugglers whom he arrested were always let off easy by the local courts, which were mostly run by members of Reverend Mather's congregation. The British government finally decided that Massachusetts would simply have to be governed in a different way. Charles II died before the plan could be worked out. The next king, James II, appointed Joseph Dudley, the son of an old Puritan governor, to head a commission, which was to run not only Massachusetts, but also New Hampshire, Maine, Rhode Island, Connecticut, New York, and New Jersey. Lumped together, they formed the Dominion of New England.

But Dudley did not last long. Tax Collector Randolph, seeing a chance to make money by selling Boston merchants the smuggled goods that he had seized, asked Dudley to cooperate with him and share in the profits. Dudley said no. Puritan leaders, anxious to do business with Randolph, were more than happy when Dudley decided to look for another job.

The Dominion of New England, through which King James II hoped to provide a better form of colonial government, was highly unpopular, especially in the Massachusetts colony. The Puritans, seeing it as a serious threat to their political power, quickly put away the "welcome mat" when Sir Edmund Andros arrived in Boston from New York to take over the job of governor. The Boston merchants, making nice profits and objecting to taxes, became worried about losing their "political connections." Worse, there was also a good chance that the Catholics might become much stronger —and where, then, would the Protestants be?

CATHOLICS PLAN INVASION OF NEW YORK

The New Englanders, along with the New Yorkers, saw the devil's hand in just about everything that Governor Andros did. Many of them claimed that his military policy was linked to a "European Catholic plot" between James II and the king of France—and even went so far as to spread the rumor that there was a similar plot to turn all of North America over to Rome.

No one could argue with them over the fact that Lord Baltimore of Maryland, Governor Thomas Dongan of New York, and Lord Howard of Virginia were all powerful Catholics.

PROTESTANTS HATED CATHOLICS, and Catholicism was a dirty word, especially in New England.

If the colonists had only known about a letter that had been sent by King Louis XIV to Count Frontenac in Montreal, they would have had still more to talk about. But, fortunately for them, Frontenac's plans for an invasion of New York in 1688 were not carried out. James II, thrown out of his kingship by an anti-Catholic Parliament, fled to France, and the British Crown was taken over jointly by two Protestants— William III, a Dutchman, and his wife, Mary. The "bloodless change," which even made the rebellion look respectable, was ever after called the "Glorious Revolution of 1688."

The New England Puritans, overjoyed by the Protestant victory in England, staged a great celebration in Boston, kicked out the Catholics who had become officeholders, and returned all of their "old crowd" to their offices. Governor Andros and his assistants were thrown into jail without the benefit of a trial. The Reverend Cotton Mather hastily drew up a "Declaration of the Gentlemen, Merchants, and Inhabitants," which put an end to the Dominion of New England in Massachusetts. Connecticut and Rhode Island followed suit, restoring their own "before-Andros" governments.

NEW YORKERS REBEL

New York, choosing a different course, reached a tragic end, partly because there was really no government for a revolution to restore, and partly because James II had become a good friend of the Courtlands, Livingstons, Van Burens, Van der Doncks, Pells, and Roosevelts, whose land holdings stretched from New York City to Albany, and whose political influence was something to be reckoned with. All of them were very much on the side of King James II.

On June 22, 1689, Lieutenant Governor Francis Nicholson, Andros's deputy for New York, called a meeting, which included delegates from New Jersey as well as New York. But Nicholson, a heavy drinker, got intoxicated during the session, threatened to burn New York City, and sparked a fight.

Jacob Leisler, a German-born merchant and captain of the local militia, stepped forward, quieted things down, and took over the job of heading a provisional government. The delegates, noting that Nicholson had "passed out," decided to give their full support to William and Mary, and appointed Leisler military commander and Acting Lieutenant Governor of New York. Sobering up, Nicholson became so mad over Leisler's taking over his job that he boarded the very next boat for London, where he planned to use influential friends to get Leisler thrown out.

But there was something that neither of the two men knew about. A letter, signed by William and Mary, was already on the way from England, announcing the appointment of Henry Sloughter, an Irish army officer, as the new governor of New York.

A Major Richard Ingoldsby, acting in the interests of Sloughter, arrived in New York ahead of the governor and demanded that Leisler step down and hand the government over to him. Leisler refused and said that

NEW YORKERS
WANTED BLOOD
and got it when the
provisional governor
was hanged by his
enemies.

he would do nothing until Sloughter arrived and took over officially. A battle followed between Ingoldsby's and Leisler's troops, and when Sloughter arrived a day or two later, Leisler was arrested and charged with high treason for having fought the king's men. He was sentenced to death and hanged by the neck on May 16, 1691, in front of City Hall in New York City. A mob, stirred up by rabble-rousers, cut him down while he was still alive and slashed his body to pieces. "The shrieks of the people," said a visitor from England, "were dreadful. . . . The crowd carried off locks of Leisler's hair and bits of his garments as souvenirs."

8
PENN'S HOLY EXPERIMENT

CHURCH WITHOUT CLERGYMEN

The son of a wealthy British admiral, William Penn, who later became the founder of Pennsylvania, was expelled from Oxford University, for having played some dirty tricks on Anglican Catholic students, and for having made some nasty remarks about the Church of England. In 1681, after having acquired a large slice of American acreage from a friend of his father, the Duke of York, Penn decided to give up the study of law to go into real estate, and to give up the life of a Puritan to become a Quaker.

The Quakers, a religious group founded by George Fox in England about 1650, had a great respect for the Bible, but chose to look for the direct word of God in the human soul. For them, no clergymen were necessary. Believing that all men were equal, they called themselves the Friends and addressed everyone as "thee" and "thou."

As Thomas E. Drake pointed out in *Quakers and Slavery in America*, the Quakers were the first religious group to speak out against slavery. Living close by the commandment "Thou shalt not kill," they were highly

AMERICANS DENIED RELIGIOUS FREEDOM: Quakers, not allowed to worship as they pleased, were often whipped, tortured, or hanged.

unpopular with many people, and with all of the war-waging governments. Over a short period of time, the Quakers moved from one place to another in the British Empire, and then went on to the Netherlands, Germany, and even Russia. In America, where religious freedom was supposed to be the order of the day, Rhode Island was the only colony that offered to take them in. Everywhere else they were either whipped or sent to jail. In New York City, they were tortured; in Boston, hanged.

If William Penn had not asked them to take part in the "holy experiment" that he had planned for his Pennsylvania colony, they might well have been forced to give up, if not die out. In Pennsylvania, they ran the place.

HYPOCRITES AND CHEATERS

The Quakers, who were far less narrow-minded than the Puritans had been in the establishment of New

England, opened the doors of Pennsylvania to all comers, no matter what their nationality, religion, or way of life happened to be. But to mean well was not enough. The Quakers, like other Christians, were sinners as well as saints and did not always practice what they preached.

As much as they talked about all men being equal, and blacks being free, they still saw fit to separate blacks from whites in their burying grounds. Out to make the mighty dollar, the Quakers saw nothing wrong in taking advantage of other freedom-seeking people who wanted to settle in Pennsylvania, charging them 15 times as much for land as the Episcopalians were charging in Virginia.

According to Samuel Eliot Morison's *Oxford History of the American People*, Penn never made a treaty with the Conestoga Indians "under the elm tree at Shacka-maxon," the scene immortalized by Benjamin West's painting. And if one had been made, it was certainly broken during the famous "walking purchase," described by Morison as "one of the slickest deals ever put over by Europeans on Indians."

To cash in on a sale made by the Conestogas to William Penn of a piece of land "as far as a man can go in a day and a half," someone thought up the cute idea of clearing a good trail and hiring three of the fastest runners in Pennsylvania, who took off early one September morning, accompanied by Quaker pacers on horseback and a few Indians to assure fair play. The Indians, after having tried to get the runners to walk, gave up in disgust before noon. As one of them said, "No sit down to smoke, no shoot squirrel, jus *lun, lun, lun* all day long." One runner quit, and the second fell into a creek and drowned. But the third, at noon of the second day, grasped a small tree, which marked the end of one and one-half day's walking. By this bit of trickery, the

Penn family got hold of half a million acres of Indian real estate.

"BROTHERLY LOVE"

King Charles II, who had been most helpful to Penn when he acquired the land for his colony, expected Pennsylvania to obey the laws of England and to pay taxes on imports. Except for their having to live up to these laws, which largely involved trade, the Pennsylvanians were pretty much free to have their own kind of government. Things went well when Penn was in Philadelphia as his own governor. But when he returned to England in 1684 to play the game of politics, and promote Quakerism, the whole colonial government came close to blowing up. Laws were broken, and there was even some smuggling of illegal goods. John Blackwell, an old soldier, whom Penn sent over from London to take over the governorship, was driven by yells and jeers from the Council chamber at Philadelphia when he tried to suggest certain reforms. Saying what he thought about the Quakers, Blackwell described them as "a people who *prayed* for their neighbors on First Day [Sunday], and *preyed* on them the other six days of the week."

Returning to Pennsylvania from England in 1699, after an absence of 15 years, Penn found himself being cheated right and left by most of his agents. None of the governors that he had appointed were any good. Upset by the way things were going, Penn wrote one of them, "For the love of God, me, and the poor country, do not be so litigious and brutish." But, surprisingly enough, Pennsylvania went on and on, and Philadelphia became known as the "City of Brotherly Love."

9

THE JEWS' TROUBLES

The Jews, who had been made to swallow the bitter pill of religious persecution the world over, looked forward to a new and better way of life in America, where everyone was supposed to be free to worship as he pleased. But, as things turned out, they found as much anti-Semitism in the New World as they had found in the Old. As Robert St. John summed it up in *Jews, Justice and Judaism*, there were all too many people who refused to accept the idea that the Jewish religion was as good as any other.

ANTI-SEMITISM IN NEW YORK

The first Jews to come to America arrived in New Amsterdam (New York City) from Brazil in September, 1654. They carried only a few personal possessions, but had the hope that here, maybe, they would be able to follow their faith freely. New Amsterdam, the capital of the Dutch colony of New Netherland, was small but cosmopolitan. Although there were fewer than a thousand settlers, one could hear no less than 18 different languages during a walk through the town.

Governed by Peter Stuyvesant, a peglegged soldier and staunch supporter of the Dutch Reformed Church, the colony was a hotbed of intolerance and prejudice, and even went so far as to throw Dutch Lutherans into jail. Baptists and Presbyterians who had been unlucky enough to drift into New Amsterdam were told to move on. Quakers, viewed as "instruments of the devil," were beaten and tortured. The Jews, noting all of these happenings, soon found out what was in store for them. On September 14, 1654, Pegleg Pete wrote to his employers, the Dutch West India Company in the Netherlands, asking for authority to kick the Jews out of New Netherland. The Reverend John Megapolensis, the head of the Dutch Reformed Church in New Amsterdam, put in his two cents' worth by writing the company that he was against allowing the Jews to become New Netherlanders, because he felt that their religion would hurt the colony spiritually, and that their "greed" would hurt it economically. Scratching away with his pen, the clergyman wrote: "These people have no other God than the Mammon of unrighteousness [riches or material wealth], and no other aim than to get possession of Christian property, and to overcome all other merchants by drawing all trade toward themselves. Therefore, we request . . . that these godless rascals, who are of no benefit to the country, may be sent away from here."

The next move came from seven Jewish leaders, all important in the commercial life of the Netherlands, who felt that they could use their influence to get the Dutch West India Company to overrule Stuyvesant. Writing to officials of the company, they pointed out that the Jews in New Amsterdam were representatives of thousands of others who had supported the Dutch against the Portuguese in Brazil, not only with their money, but also with their lives. The Dutch West India Company finally gave in, telling Stuyvesant: ". . . we have decided that these Brazilian Jews may travel and

JEWS PERSECUTED IN NEW AMSTERDAM: Jewish settlers were not allowed to earn a living and were forced to live in ghettos.

trade . . . in New Netherland, and live and remain there, providing that the poor among them shall not become a burden to the company or to the community. . . ."

Overruled as he was, Stuyvesant still went right on making life as difficult as he could for the Jewish immigrants. Their houses, forming a ghetto which came to be known as Jews' Alley, had to be built "as close together as possible." As if this were not bad enough, they were also forbidden to open retail stores or to work at trades of any kind. But, by far, the severest blow was the news that the Jews would not be allowed to build a synagogue, or even pray together in public. Only the Dutch Reformed Church had the right to build religious buildings, and hold public gatherings. The Jews, forced to hold secret religious services in private homes, were no better off in America than they had been in Brazil or anywhere else.

LEVY STRIKES BACK

Luckily for the Jews, they found a leader in Asser Levy, a fur trader and a former resident of the

BEATING THE DUTCH: Asser Levy, the first Jew to own American real estate, fought for his right to citizenship and won his case.

Netherlands, who became the first Jew to own real estate in the New World. Objecting to a discriminating military tax, Levy demanded that he have the right to stand guard in defense of the colony, like any other citizen. The judges of the local court not only turned him down, but also told him that if he did not like their decision, he was hereby given permission "to depart whenever and whither it pleases him." Not a man to give up easily, Levy continued to do guard duty every night, and 18 months later, he finally won his case. From that day on, the Jews had "rights," if only to stand guard.

THE BRITISH TAKE OVER

In 1664, 10 years after the first Jews arrived in New Amsterdam, a fleet of British warships dropped anchor in the same harbor. Peter Stuyvesant, as poor a general as he was a governor, surrendered the entire settlement without firing a shot. Almost overnight, the Dutch colony of New Netherland became the British colony of New York.

The English, more tolerant than the Dutch, offered religious freedom to all Christians. The Jews, on the other hand, had to wait for many years before they could likewise benefit from the royal order which read: "All persons of what Religion soever were guaranteed against any disturbance or disquiet whatsoever for and by reason of their differing opinions in matters of Religion, as long as they did not disturb the public peace or molest others in ye free exercise of their Religion." It was not until 1730 that the New York Jews were able to build their first synagogue. Known as the Shearith Israel, it was located in the downtown section of New York City.

But even with this "official recognition" of their religion, the Jews still found it difficult to increase their number in early America. By 1776, when the total population of the 13 colonies tallied close to two and a half million, there were no more than two or three thousand Jewish residents. Maybe this was why they managed to escape some of the bad treatment that was so often meted out to the Catholics and Quakers. Or maybe it was because they were not looked upon so often as "public enemies." About the worst thing that the Protestants wanted to do to them was to "convert" them to Christianity.

IO

REVOLUTIONARY SCHEMERS

The 13 American colonies, having fought the French and shared the glory of victory with Great Britain at the end of the so-called French and Indian War in 1763, were more than pleased to belong to the British Empire. King George III was as popular in America as he was in Great Britain. The American colonists, then the freest people in the world, gave vent to their patriotic feelings and fairly slopped over with loyalty to the Crown. But, as so often happens in the closest of families, the day came when there were heated arguments over money. The mother country, deeply in debt because of the war, and badly in need of cash to provide military protection for her colonies, expected the Americans to join with other Britishers, and pay their share of the bill. But as many historians have pointed out, the Americans refused not only to pay taxes, but also to obey British laws.

King George III, knowing how bitterly the Indians already felt about the increased use of British axes and plows on their land, issued the Proclamation of 1763, forbidding the settlement of any territory west of the Appalachian Mountains. The proclamation did not rest too well with the frontier farmers, land speculators, and colonial merchants who wanted to move into the "Old West" or "back country" that stretched from Virginia to the Carolinas.

SHADY DEALINGS IN REAL ESTATE

George Washington, a Virginia plantation owner, who had served as a British colonel in the French and Indian War, decided to pay no attention to what the king had said. Expressing his feelings to his friend William Crawford about a large piece of Pennsylvania real estate that the two of them had planned to grab for themselves, Washington wrote: "I can never look on that proclamation in any other light (but this I say between ourselves) than as a temporary expedient to quiet the minds of the Indians and must fall, of course, in a few years. . . . Any person therefore who neglects the present opportunity of hunting out good lands, and in some measure marking . . . them for their own (in order to keep others from settling them), will never regain it. . . . The scheme must be snugly carried on by you under the pretence of hunting other game."

This sort of thing went on all along the frontier, with "hunters" roaming the woods and "marking trees." The Vandalia Company, a large land-speculating organization promoted by Benjamin Franklin, even went so far as to use "political connections" in London to try to get millions of acres of land in the Ohio Valley for almost nothing. The British Board of Trade and Plantations finally wrecked the schemes of the American land speculators by clamping down on their political friends in England. Without a doubt, this did much to cause many of the schemers to favor an independent American government, which might look more kindly on their real estate plans.

57

ROUGHHOUSE TACTICS

The American colonists, rallying around the slogan "No taxation without representation," began to show signs of colonial patriotism. Organizing themselves into activist groups under the banner of the Sons of Liberty, they decided that nothing would sting the mother country more deeply than the loss of money, via a boycott of all British goods. Colonists who did not observe the ban were beaten up by the Sons of Liberty, and coated with tar and feathers.

In Boston, where the fiercest opposition to Britain's tax laws took place, a militant group, led by Samuel Adams, an ex-tax collector, and John Hancock, a local merchant, conducted a campaign that skillfully combined violence with legal and political strategy. By the late 1760's, radicals were seated not only in the elected Massachusetts Assembly, but also in the executive Council that ran the colony.

Faced with the pressure of the "liberty mobs," Britain had reacted with a great deal of tolerance. From 1770 on, there were no British taxes on any British goods except for a small tax on tea. But this, too, was to be kept on the boycott list of the Sons of Liberty.

BLOODTHIRSTY BOSTONIANS

On March 5, 1770, a big brawl broke out in Boston. A gang of waterside toughs, described by John Adams, a cousin of Samuel Adams, as "Negroes and mulattoes, Irish rowdies, and outlandish sailors," began pelting with snowballs a British soldier who was on guard duty at the custom house on King (now State) Street. The main guard, consisting of some 20 men, was called out and, with fixed bayonets, faced up to the yelling lawless mob. After the soldiers had been yelled at and snowballed for half an hour, one of them, who had been hit with a club, lost his "cool" and fired his rifle. Other soldiers

BRUTALITY WAS THE ORDER OF THE DAY: Colonists, caught with British goods, were beaten up, and coated with tar and feathers.

followed suit; and when the smoke cleared away, three members of the gang (one a black sailor named Crispus Attucks) lay dead, and two mortally wounded.

As the drums beat out for a full regimental turnout, Thomas Hutchinson, the royal governor, appeared, and order was restored. One of the mortally wounded men, speaking from his deathbed, said that he had seen mobs in Ireland, but never knew troops to bear so much without firing as these had done. The soldiers, who were charged with murder, hired John Adams as their lawyer. Obtaining their acquittal, Adams wrote: "Judgement of death against these Soldiers would have been as foul a Stain upon this Country as the Executions of the Quakers . . . recently." The Sons of Liberty, angered by the court's decision, described the affair as a "wanton killing of peaceable citizens," and called it the "Boston Massacre."

America rang with outraged cries. There were strong hints from London suggesting that the radicals pipe down.

But Samuel Adams, in no mood to take any advice

from Britishers, squeezed out every ounce of propaganda that he could from the "massacre." With his pen fairly flying over paper, he wrote a "martyr" version of the story, which appeared in all of the colonial newspapers. On each succeeding Fifth of March—until the Fourth of July replaced it—the Sons of Liberty staged "memorial processions and demonstrations" to keep the fires of turmoil burning.

MONEY TALKED

John Hancock, enjoying an increased retail business as a result of Parliament's doing away with many taxes, told Governor Hutchinson that he was finished with the Sons of Liberty, and that he would have nothing more to do with agitation. John Adams penned in his diary: "I shall certainly become more retired and cautious; I shall certainly mind my own farm and my own business." Benjamin Franklin, taking care of colonial business in England, begged his fellow Americans to keep quiet, pointing out that the British government had made some great concessions, and that America "could well afford to bear the slight tax burden still placed upon her."

Samuel Adams, worried over the way things were going, wrote one of his friends in the Sons of Liberty: "It is to be feared that the people will be so accustomed to bondage as to forget they were ever free. . . . Every day strengthens our opponents and weakens us."

TEMPEST OVER TEA

The tax on tea did not seem to bother American colonial tea drinkers too much. Between the years 1768–72, they consumed close to two million pounds of legally imported tea, plus whatever they managed to get from smugglers. The British government, hopeful of helping the East India Company out of its financial difficulties,

**RADICALS WENT WILD, and, by staging the "Boston Tea Party,"
goaded Great Britain into a showdown.**

legalized a new arrangement in 1773, which removed
the tax on tea entering England and allowed the company to be its own exporter to the 13 colonies, doing
away with middlemen. This added no new tax, but took
one off; and, if enforced, it would enable the company
to undersell the smugglers and give colonial consumers a
cheaper cup of tea.

It was difficult to find anything legally wrong with
this arrangement—but Samuel Adams still wrote articles
for the newspapers about the "illegal monopoly" that
had been given to the East India Company. So, when the
tea ships began to arrive in American ports in
December, 1773, the Sons of Liberty were ready. In
Charleston, the tea was locked up in vaults; at New

61

York and Philadelphia the captains of the ships were "persuaded" to turn back without entering the harbors; in Boston, where the Sons of Liberty had been upset by a criticism that "Bostonians were better at deciding what to do than doing what they decided," excitement ran especially high.

On the night of December 16, 1773, a mob of about 50 men, led by Samuel Adams, disguised themselves as Mohawk Indians and blacks, boarded the two tea ships in the harbor, broke open 342 large cases of precious tea, and threw them overboard. Someone, possibly Samuel Adams himself, shouted, "Boston Harbor is a teapot this night!"

The Boston Tea Party, as this comic opera was called, goaded Great Britain into a showdown, which was exactly what Samuel Adams and the Sons of Liberty wanted.

The British, in reply, closed Boston harbor until the Bostonians chose to pay for the tumbled tea, revised the government of Massachusetts, provided for trial in England for persons charged with capital crimes, and authorized the housing of British troops in colonial homes. Linked with these laws, but really directed toward an entirely different problem, was the Quebec Act, which extended the boundaries of Canada over the entire territory north of the Ohio River, and west of the Allegheny Mountains, thereby preventing the westward expansion of the Atlantic seaboard colonies.

From the time that these laws were passed in London, the question between England and the 13 American colonies was mainly one of power. Who would rule, or have the final say? And who would dictate the terms of their mutual association, or separation?

II
INDEPENDENCE DECLARED

The Declaration of Independence, the sacred document by which 13 British colonies became the United States of America, sought not only to justify the American Revolution, but also to put all of the blame on King George III for everything that had gone wrong between America and Great Britain. While the document states certain "self-evident truths," it does not prove them, nor, in fact, could they have been proved. Some of these "truths" were falsified even as they were being put down on paper.

Alleged to be man's God-given rights were life, liberty, and equality. Yet, the newspapers of the day carried copies of the Declaration along with advertisements promoting the sale of slaves. The idea that governments derive their "just powers from the consent of the governed" had yet to be realized. Significant for what it left out, the document carried no mention of Parliament (Great Britain's legislature), slavery, or what had been so often talked about by the American colonists: the rights of British subjects. But, with independence well under way, there was no longer any need for the men who signed it to think like Englishmen. The whole case for independence could now be placed on the higher level of the "rights of man."

In the eyes of the Britishers, the Declaration was but one more act of treason by the American rebels. Those loyal to the king were Tories, and no longer merely men who did not happen to agree with the Whigs, or patriots; *they* were traitors. For them, the period of tar and feathers was over; their punishment would be death. Some 100,000 Loyalists fled to Canada to save their necks.

EQUAL BUT UNEQUAL

The introduction to the Declaration of Independence, clothed in the flowery language of Thomas Jefferson, contains the "meat" of the popular document: the belief that "all men are created equal." But Jefferson never meant to include blacks when he wrote it. Because, if he had, he would have had to ask how that harmonized with the fact that, at that very moment, there were 500,000 slaves in America. What a pity that Jefferson and his fellow members of the Continental Congress did not put in a few lines that would have ended the slave trade. By so doing, they could have stamped out slavery almost one hundred years before the Emancipation Proclamation. Jefferson himself used slaves on his Virginia plantation.

Commenting on the Declaration, David Cooper, a Quaker antislaver, wrote: "If these solemn *truths*, uttered at such an awful crisis, are *self-evident*: unless we can shew that the African race are not *men*, words can hardly express the amazement which naturally arises on reflecting, that the very people who make these pompous declarations are slaveholders, and, by their legislative conduct, tell us, that these blessings were only meant to be the *rights* of *white men* not of all *men*: and would seem to verify the observation of an eminent writer; 'When men talk of liberty, they mean their own liberty, and seldom suffer their thoughts on that point to stray to their neighbours.' "

Slavery was in no way thought about in the American Revolution. But, when it ended, Cooper said, "We need not now turn over the libraries of Europe for authorities to prove that blacks are born equally with whites: it is declared and recorded as the sense of America."

THE RIGHT TO LIVE

Jefferson's line about the right to "life, liberty, and the pursuit of happiness" was later ridiculed by Oliver Wendell Holmes, an Associate Justice of the United States Supreme Court. As he pointed out: "Even before the adoption of military conscription . . . soldiers were marched off to fight without any thought of a supposed right to life. The most fundamental of the rights—the right to life—is sacrificed without a scruple, not only in war, but whenever the interest of society . . . is thought to demand it."

The same famous judge made a similar observation on the use of the word "liberty": "Law is inherently a restraint of liberty. . . . Every restraint which men are laid under by a state or government is a privation of their natural rights. . . . Civil liberty includes religious freedom, the rights of thinking, speaking, forming and giving opinions, and perhaps all these can be fully exercised by the individual without the aid of exterior assistance."

As for the phrase "pursuit of happiness," Holmes saw it as a "salad of fancy words," the idea already having been covered by "liberty."

"PEOPLE," NOT ALL PEOPLE

The American rebels based their case for rebellion on the need of the people for a government "deriving" its "just powers from the consent of the governed." But, in 1776, the word "people" was rather narrow in meaning. Slaves were not considered people; nor were men who did not own property. To be a person whose voice counted in public affairs, one had to be white, a holder of property, a taxpayer, and a Christian, preferably a Protestant.

The Declaration, as it was written, carries the title: "The unanimous Declaration of the thirteen united States of America." But this seems to have raised a question. Was the Declaration an act of the people of the 13 colonies, or an act of the people of America? In later years, this question became a matter of great importance, brought up often by lawyers who argued for states' rights, and by those who argued for a strong central government.

A SOURCE OF WORRY

The Declaration of Independence, officially adopted by the Continental Congress on July 4, 1776, became a serious source of worry for many of the leading patriots. Alarmed over the tendency toward "anarchy and confusion," George Washington feared that liberty, "the foundation on which the glorious fabric of our Independency and National Character must be supported," would be weakened or destroyed. He then went on to say, "I do not conceive we can long last as a nation without having lodged somewhere a power which will pervade the whole Union in as energetic a manner as the authority of the state governments extend over the several states."

Alexander Hamilton, in complete agreement with Washington, warned that great changes were "necessary to save us from ruin." Noting that "the inefficiency of our government becomes daily more and more apparent," John Jay confessed that he was "uneasy and

AMERICANS DENIED RIGHT TO VOTE: This, as well as the right to hold public office, was for property owners only.

apprehensive." John Adams, also worried over the way things were going, said that he was "afraid that the Republic would not last beyond his lifetime."

12
THE PATRIOTS

George Washington, who has been highly praised by many people for serving as Commander-in-Chief of the Continental Army without pay, actually did rather well for himself in the American Revolution. As Marvin Kitman pointed out in *George Washington's Expense Account,* if General Washington had gone on the army payroll like other patriot generals, he would have collected a mere $48,000 for his eight years' service. But, with his expense account arrangement, he not only made future generals look like pikers, but also established a guideline for future "big spenders." His vouchers, approved for payment by the Continental Congress, added up to $449,261.50, or over $56,000 a year, tax free. Satisfied with nothing but the best in clothes, food, drink, shelter, and horses, he lived almost as well in war as he did in peace.

THE GENERAL'S LADIES

A love affair, reportedly carried on by General Washington and Mary Gibbons, a British informer in New York City, could have resulted in his loss of the war and of his faithful wife, Martha. Miss Gibbons, learning much about Washington's military plans during

68

WASHINGTON WENT IN FOR SEX and could have lost the war by playing around as much as he did.

the nights he spent with her, passed on everything that she knew to William Tryon, the royal governor of New York, who later led a number of raids on American seaport towns, destroying badly needed supplies.

Mrs. Robert Murray, another of Washington's lady friends, was said to have saved the general's neck after the Battle of Long Island in 1776, when she used her "charms" to make British General William Howe forget the war long enough to enable Washington to plan a successful retreat from Manhattan Island (Washington Heights) to White Plains, New York. Murray Hill, a section of New York City, was named after her.

AN UNPOPULAR ARMY

Washington had scarcely taken command of the Continental Army in Boston in 1775 when he was asked to discharge the Massachusetts patriots who had fought the British in the Battle of Breed's Hill (not Bunker's, as reported in many history books). The New Englanders, like other Americans, were opposed to standing armies and long-term enlistments. Many men refused to sign up with the Continental Army for even one year; few, if any, were willing to re-enlist. Northerners would not go south to fight; Southerners would not go north. At harvest time it was not unusual for a soldier to desert a battlefield so that he could go home to take care of a cornfield.

The general's officers, mostly militiamen, were no more patriotic than the men who served under them. Making good use of friends in Congress, they managed to get promotions whether they were entitled or not. Troops from one state would not obey officers from another state. General Benedict Arnold, denouncing the ". . . tyranny and injustice of Congress," and angry over the unfair treatment that he got from General Horatio Gates in the Battle of Saratoga, turned traitor and went over to the British side. A small group of officers, playing military politics, even went so far as to try to get General Washington replaced by General Gates. In 1778, when France joined America as an ally, many officers, along with the men under them, wanted to quit and let the French finish the fight.

The officer problem was further complicated by foreign volunteers, most of whom arrived in army camps without knowing a word of English. Unemployed professional soldiers, kept idle by 12 years of peace in Europe, were more than anxious to serve in the Continental Army. Tired of their daily visits to his Paris office, Benjamin Franklin decided to get rid of these professionals by giving them free passage to America and a letter of introduction to the president of the Continental Congress. Appointed to ranks as high as major general, many of them did nothing except to tell General Washington in French, German, or Polish that his troops were lousy.

MUTINY COMES IN TO PLAY

General Anthony Wayne's Pennsylvanians, angered by a Massachusetts colonel who saw fit to allow officers to mix with enlisted men, attacked the colonel's headquarters, driving his men from their tents with gunfire. A mutiny of the New Jerseyans had to be put down by six hundred troops from other states. A near-mutiny by the Connecticut Yankees, stationed at Washington's headquarters in Morristown, New Jersey, in 1780, was squelched by a Pennsylvania regiment, which itself mutinied the next year, killing several officers.

CREDIT PROBLEMS

One of the main reasons why Washington's army, at Valley Forge and later, went unfed, unclothed, and unshod was no lack of supplies in the country, but the unwillingness of money-hungry suppliers to exchange food, clothing, and boots for Continental notes. The merchants of Philadelphia, in 1781, refused to furnish General Nathanael Greene with much-needed clothing for the Southern army, although they had the cloth, and the general signed a note for the money. Europe was used to armies helping themselves in wartime, and collecting from the government later; but in free colonial America, the people would not do such a thing, and Washington was forced to "forage the country naked."

COLOR BARS

There had been no color line in the French and Indian War (1755–63), but the Continental Army and Navy, initially at least, refused to accept blacks for fear of a slave rebellion. Despite this, the need of men to fill the ranks eventually pulled both slaves and free blacks into the armed forces, many of them clutching the promise of freedom as their reward for fighting for it. Rhode Island organized a "separate battalion" of blacks. In South Carolina, where John Laurens suggested that black troops be organized, the state legislature turned thumbs down on the idea. Virginia went wild with anger when John Murray Dunmore, the royal governor, issued a notice from aboard a British warship, offering freedom to all blacks who were willing to fight for King George III. Georgia, the most stubborn of all of the states, held out against slave enlistment until the end of the war.

MORE TALK THAN ACTION

Patriot leaders—including Thomas Jefferson, the Cabots and Lodges of Boston, and most of the signers of the Declaration of Independence—were quick to use their tongues and pens against the British, but never carried a rifle in the entire war. John Hancock, the president of the Continental Congress, showed up at one battle in Rhode Island in 1781, and then returned to Boston, where he "did business as usual."

In his book, *Code Number 72 / Benjamin Franklin: Patriot or Spy?*, historian Cecil B. Currey raised the possibility that Franklin may not have been the wholly shining patriot talked about in American history. Basing his case on what he described as "previously unused papers of the British Secret Service," the author concluded that in the delicate negotiation period of 1776–85, when Franklin was America's ambassador to France, the master diplomat "may indeed have been an enemy agent."

The British, knowing that the 13 American states were doing a lot of bickering among themselves, hoped that they would splinter apart naturally and merely

BLACKS REJECTED: The Continental Army and Navy turned blacks down and accepted only whites, in the early part of the war.

need sweeping up. Only the entrance of the French and the Spanish on the side of the Americans made the British finally lose the war. The French Navy, controlling Virginia waters, forced the surrender of British General Charles Cornwallis at Yorktown in 1781.

The peace treaty that followed recognized the independence of the United States of America, whose territory now stretched south from the Great Lakes and east from the Mississippi River. Great Britain retained her rights in West Florida, but this thorn in the southern end of America was soon restored to Spain. Proposals for free trade between America and Britain came to nothing, because neither of them felt that the other could be trusted. America, taking a close look at her allies, France and Spain, began to consider how far she would have to go to take over their possessions in the New World.

13

A GOVERNMENT IS CONSTITUTED

The American Constitution, written by men of property for men of property, did a rather good job of welding the original 13 "Free and Independent States" into a "more perfect union." But, in truth, it was actually no more or no less than the Founding Fathers claimed it to be: a formula for a system of government suited to the "needs of the moment." It was not written, as George Washington himself had demanded, "to please the people." Out of the 55 men who met in Philadelphia in 1787 to draw up the Constitution, only 39 were willing to sign it. Fortunately, Richard Henry Lee and a few others, opposed to a strong central government, insisted that a Bill of Rights be added to the document to protect individuals against "governmental tyranny." Otherwise, such rights as freedom of speech and freedom of religion would not have been provided for.

If Thomas Jefferson had had his way, a complete revision of the Constitution—at least once in a generation—would have been required by law. James Madison, one of the chief architects of the document, never thought that it would last so long as to become the moss-covered, out-of-date instrument of government

CONSTITUTION VIEWED AS IMPERFECT: Jefferson, Madison, and Hamilton were all critical of the Constitution, and expected it to be revised or superseded.

that it is today. Alexander Hamilton described it as "a weak and worthless fabric, certain to be superseded." Indeed, there have been many amendments—some that turned out to be good and some that turned out to be bad—to adapt the document to changing social requirements. But, with all of these changes, it has become little more than a tangled mass of contradictory decrees, many of which make little or no sense in present-day society. Many authorities on government say that the nation is overdue for a completely new Constitution.

PROPERTY ALL-IMPORTANT

The Founding Fathers, equating ownership with joy, considered property to be of the utmost importance. Jefferson, pursuing noble principles while authoring the Declaration of Independence, had defined the chief rights of men as "life, liberty, and the pursuit of happiness"; the Founding Fathers, taking a slightly different point of view while authoring the Constitution, defined them as "life, liberty, and property." They were willing enough to consider the idea of equality among men, but were completely unwilling to part with any of their own riches and power in the process of doing so.

As Madison put it, "equality of property would make way for a 'leveling' of society that would serve to drag down the good rather than elevate the bad."

Alexis de Tocqueville, the French statesman and author, later confirmed the attitude of the Founding Fathers when he reported that he had never visited a country outside of America "where the love of money has taken a stronger hold on the affections of men. . . ."

PRESIDENTIAL POWER

The Constitution, written in loose language, states that "The Executive power shall be vested in a President of the United States," but, departing from this generality, it goes on to itemize a number of functions that fall within the scope of Presidential authority. And, to make things more confusing, the President is made a "partner" in the legislative process by giving him the power to veto measures, which can only be overridden by a two-thirds vote of both the Senate and the House of Representatives.

Thus some Presidents have been described as "weak," because they have confined themselves to exercising the powers itemized by the Constitution, and Congress has been the dominating branch of government in their time. Others, described as "strong" Presidents, have continually increased their executive power by reading "inherent" authorities into their oath of office as well as into the Constitution itself. The Supreme Court, professing its inability to prohibit a President from exceeding his constitutional powers, even when the Court seems to be right, expressed the view that in such cases the Chief Executive was "accountable only to the country and to his conscience."

The President, named Commander-in-Chief of the armed forces by the Constitution, partly to ensure civilian control of the military, has always had the power to act quickly when he needed to. Congress, a deliberative body, moves more slowly and cautiously. From President Thomas Jefferson's Louisiana Purchase to President Lyndon Baines Johnson's dispatch of troops to Vietnam, the Chief Executive has largely taken the lead in foreign and military policies, while Congress has tagged along, often finding fault. When an earlier power-happy President, James K. Polk, sent troops into Mexico, and then demanded that Congress approve his action, Senator John C. Calhoun of South Carolina declared that the deed "stripped Congress of its constitutional power to make war, and what was more and worse, it gave that power to every officer, nay, to every subaltern commanding a corporal's guard." As before and since, the President got away with it.

To protect the very heart of the Constitution, the principle of the separation of powers among the Executive, Legislative, and Judicial branches, the Founding Fathers built a wall so high and so wide that trespass by any of the three in the province of another would provide grounds for a limited, if not an all-out departmental war. Yet, even popular Presidents with party majorities on Capitol Hill have been forced by Congress or the federal courts into courses they opposed, or have been denied approval of legislation to which they brought the powerful pressures inherent in their office. Congressman Henry Clay of Kentucky and his followers forced a most unwilling President James Madison into the War of 1812. Congressional "war hawks," making the most out of jingo sentiments, literally pushed President William McKinley into the Spanish-American War in 1898.

THE VICE PRESIDENT—IMPORTANT OR IMPOTENT?

Describing Vice Presidents, President Harry S. Truman said that they were "about as useful as a cow's fifth teat." Woodrow Wilson's Vice President, Thomas R. Marshall, remarked: "Once there were two brothers. One ran away to sea, the other was elected Vice President, and nothing was ever heard of either of them again."

Something of that attitude has continued to persist in the nation's political machinery. What other reason would the parties have for locating and ratifying their Vice Presidential choices so haphazardly, and with so little foresight? Yet the Vice Presidency is by no means a meaningless office. Twelve of the nation's 36 Presidents got their training in that capacity; eight of them stepped into a dead President's shoes.

Originally, the Constitution provided for the electoral runner-up in a Presidential election to become Vice President. But, in 1800, Thomas Jefferson and Aaron Burr tied in electoral votes for the Presidency, throwing the election into the House of Representatives. That experience brought about the 12th Amendment to the Constitution in 1804, by which the present method of Vice Presidential selection was introduced.

The system has not been a total disaster. Political scientist Paul Halpern of the University of California in Los Angeles feels that it has actually produced favorable surprises, such as Theodore Roosevelt and Harry S. Truman. On the other hand, it has also handed up a succession of faceless mediocrities.

ELECTORAL DISTORTION

There is nothing in the Constitution to prevent a "runaway" Electoral College from completely thwarting the will of a majority of the people in a Presidential election. As pointed out by Kenneth B. Keating in *Government of the People*, there have been a number of proposals for remedying the present Electoral College system, but only a direct election by popular vote would achieve the objectives of meaningful reform. Under the direct election system, every citizen in every part of the nation would speak with an equal voice, and exercise the same weight in the choice of a President. The guiding principle would be "one American, one vote," as it should be in a modern democracy.

Commenting on the election of 1960, when John F. Kennedy defeated Richard M. Nixon, the noted syndicated columnist Roscoe Drummond wrote in a column in the *Washington Post*:

> The election has proved how dangerous to the democratic process the electoral system can be. It has shown that even though we are agreed on majority rule, the Electoral College can put in the White House the minority candidate.
>
> My plea that we free ourselves from the tentacles of the electoral system does not rest primarily on what might have happened to the candidates; it rests primarily on what might have happened to the right of the American people to pick their President by majority vote. This election has shown again how the electoral-vote system is a one-way street with a built-in trap door through which the will of the American people can disappear at any time.
>
> I am not suggesting that there is some magic wisdom in the judgment of the majority. Obviously the majority could choose the less qualified candidate. But, unless you want to suspend our democracy, is there any better way of choosing the President? Do we want to leave the outcome of our elections either to whim or to accident?
>
> If we believe that the popular will should prevail in picking the President, we had better do something about the Electoral College.

CONGRESS ENFEEBLED: With legislators doing little or nothing to check the power of the President, many Americans fear that the United States could become an "Executive monarchy," even under the Constitution.

THE CONGRESS SLOWLY SURRENDERING

The Congress of the United States, intended by the writers of the Constitution to be the nation's supreme policy setter, lawmaker, and reflector of the collective will of the American people, has been surrendering its powers for many years. Although it is still to be broken, it has been severely bent, and in danger of cracking. Despite North Carolina's Senator Sam Ervin's picturing it as "the most powerful political legislative body on the face of the earth," and Tennessee's Senator William Brock's calling it "one of the most remarkable institutions known to man," Congress has been failing miserably, and no longer effectively checks the President, as required by the Constitution.

Oregon's Senator Robert W. Packwood, envisioning

Congress's becoming a mere "vetoing agency" and having the ability only to object to Presidential initiatives, feared that the United States would wind up with a government "very close to an Executive monarchy." Abraham Ribicoff, who served as President John F. Kennedy's Secretary of Health, Education and Welfare before he became a United States Senator from Connecticut, saw Pennsylvania Avenue as "a one-way street, with all the power flowing from a White House that invariably lies to the Congress, massages it, and seduces it to get its will." Giving his view of the legislative branch of government while writing *Congress: The Sapless Branch*, Joseph S. Clark, a United States Senator from Pennsylvania for 12 years, and, before that, mayor of Philadelphia, said:

> Whether we look at city councils, the state legislatures, or the Congress of the United States, we react to what we see with scarcely concealed contempt. This is the area where democratic government is breaking down. This is where the vested-interest lobbies tend to run riot, where conflict of interest is concealed from the public. . . . I have no hesitation in stating my deep conviction that the legislatures of America, local, state, and national, are presently the greatest menace in our country to the successful operation of the democratic process.

In its earlier days, Congress had a lot less cause to quarrel with the White House than it has had in the 20th century. The President, elected indirectly by what was then a truly independent Electoral College, existed almost solely to carry out the will of Congress. Looked upon as a national administrator, he did not even dare to veto a piece of legislation he personally opposed, unless he believed that by signing it he would violate his oath to uphold the Constitution. The early fights came instead between the Congressmen, elected by popular vote in their home districts, and the Senators, who were then selected by state legislatures. The House of Representatives may have been, as Alexis de Tocqueville said, "remarkable for its vulgarity and its poverty of talent." But it was dominant, having the sole power to introduce revenue legislation, and impeach federal officials, including the President. The Senate's role, as Alexander Hamilton described it, was "to correct the prejudices, check the intemperate passions, and regulate the fluctuations of the more democratic House."

The erosion of House dominance began when Andrew Jackson was elected President in 1828. Jackson thought up the argument that he was "the only representative of all the people." He also introduced the idea of the "spoils system," or political patronage, thereby enhancing the role of the Senate, which alone had the power to approve or reject Presidential appointees. The heated debates over slavery that took place before the War Between the States were staged in the Senate rather than in the House, which was greatly divided over the issue. Yet, even President Abraham Lincoln, who devised the masterly political gambit of the Emancipation Proclamation, sometimes deferred to Capitol Hill. Said he: "Congress should originate, as well as perfect, its measures without external bias."

The War Between the States helped to create a strong two-party system, in which a succession of powerful House Speakers used positions of party leadership to restore the supremacy of that chamber. These men—first James G. Blane, then Samuel J. Randall, John G. Carlisle, and finally Thomas B. Reed —appointed committee chairmen, dictated legislative priorities, and determined the fate of their bills by the simple exercise of their power of recognizing their favorites on the floor. By 1890, Reed was so contemptuous of the White House that he refused President Benjamin Harrison's invitations to discuss his Congressional plans. It was Reed who told a fellow Congressman in 1892: "I have been 15 years in Congress, and I never saw a Speaker's decision overruled, and you will never live to see it either."

The need for Congressmen to be forever seeking re-election has been severely criticized by many authorities on government, although some political scientists have argued that it actually keeps them better informed on the desires of their constituents than any other federal officials. Also criticized was the dependence of many legislators on campaign contributions from contributors with special interests. Senator Walter F. Mondale of Minnesota called this "the dark side of the political moon, tragic and dangerous." Senator William B. Saxbe of Ohio said that a contributor almost always expects a return favor. "It is like the boy who buys a girl a beer, and then expects to squeeze it out of her."

The only law governing the conduct of Congressmen is the out-of-date—and universally ignored—Corrupt Practices Act, which was passed by Congress in 1925—long before the costs of radio and television advertising made political campaigns soar beyond the means of all but the wealthiest candidates. It demands that Congressmen file a record of their personal campaign expenses, and that committees operating in more than one state also file reports. To circumvent this, legislators set up committees in their states to handle their financing. Such a gimmick enabled Senator Edward M. Kennedy of Massachusetts to report both contributions and expenses at zero after his costly 1964 campaign. Under the terms of the law, he was able to say he neither collected nor paid out a penny; all transactions were handled by campaign committees.

As Charles Jones, the author of *Minority Party Leadership in Congress*, observed: "Whatever is wrong with Congress may also reflect ills in the society. And if the legislature fails, democracy fails."

THE COSTLY SUPREME COURT

The concept of "liberty and justice for all," expressed in the pledge of allegiance to the flag of the United States, is most decisively mocked by the high cost of taking a conviction up to the Supreme Court on appeal. Most of the cases handled by the Justices carry the price tags of expensive contests at law. Though the Supreme Court's civil and human rights decisions are usually well publicized, such cases are actually in a minority on the Court's calendar. Carrying an appeal all the way up to the nation's highest court costs something in the neighborhood of $30,000. Only a well-to-do American can afford to do it. A large corporation, for example, can readily fork up the money to pay the fees of legal researchers, consultants, or even an entire law firm. A small-time litigant, on the other hand, has all that he can do to get inside any courtroom.

There have been numerous proposals introduced in Congress "to do something about the Supreme Court." These vary from impeachment resolutions to suggestions that the Constitution be amended to make the Justices elective, to bills depriving the Court of jurisdiction to hear cases involving threats to national security. But, up to now, nothing has been done.

14
WASHINGTON AS PRESIDENT

America's future was none too secure on April 30, 1789, when George Washington, the leader of the Federalist party, stepped onto the balcony of Federal Hall, on New York City's Wall Street, to be sworn in as President of the United States. The nation was more "disunited" than "united." The enemies of the Constitution were numerous and powerful. The drift of opinion was toward state power rather than federal power. There were no more than 400,000 free adult men —perhaps one out of seven—in the total population of the 13 states, and only one out of three of them had the right to vote or hold public office. Women, children, servants, all non-Christians, Indians, and slaves were all treated as second-class citizens.

Society, outside of the backwoods and cities along the Atlantic Coast, was controlled by the wealthy, many of whom had good reason to live with fear in the newly created republic. City mobs, rebelling against poverty, threatened the destruction of businesses and the homes of the rich; poor farmers and mechanics, unable to pay taxes and other bills, and led by insurrectionists such as Daniel Shays of Massachusetts, took up arms to rebel

TROUBLE: City mobs, rebelling against poverty, threatened the destruction of businesses and homes of the wealthy.

against state governments that refused to give them any help or relief.

Attempting to appease the Democratic-Republican party, which was opposed to a strong central government, President Washington asked Congress to add the Bill of Rights to the Constitution to protect the religious freedom and rights of the individual, including his rights to free speech, reasonable bail, speedy trial, and the possession of firearms. But, even when this was done, the Democratic-Republicans were still far from satisfied.

Patrick Henry, representing the state of Virginia, was against the federal government's having the right to collect taxes and wanted this to be left to the states. William Grayson, Henry's fellow representative, screamed for a new Constitution and sneered at the Bill of Rights, claiming that they were "good for nothing." Massachusetts, which started this whole movement in the first place, did nothing about adopting the Bill of Rights until 150 years later, when someone discovered the oversight.

WHY NOT A MONARCHY?

As Alpheus Thomas Mason and Richard H. Leach pointed out in their book, *In Quest of Freedom: American Political Thought and Practice*, there were many Americans —particularly New Englanders—who favored a monarchy over a republican form of government.

Nathaniel Gorham, a member of Congress representing the state of Massachusetts, even went so far as to write German Prince Henry of Brandenberg, suggesting that he accept an American kingship, but, fortunately, the prince politely turned down the invitation.

John Adams, Washington's Vice President, felt that no republic could be "respectable" without royalty. Senator William Maclay of Pennsylvania was shocked at Adams's referring to the President's inaugural address as "His Most Gracious Speech," and reminded the Senate that "the removal of royal trimmings" was one of the main reasons for America's having fought Great Britain in the American Revolution. The Vice President "expressed the greatest surprise that anything should be objected to on account of its being taken from the practice of that government under which we had lived so long and happily formerly; that he was for a dignified and respectable government"; but the phrase was struck out of the Senate record.

Later, a Senate committee reported that the Chief Executive should be addressed as "His Highness the President of the United States of America and the Protector of the rights of the Same." The House of Representatives, more democratic than the Senate, refused to agree; and Washington, along with his successors, remained plain "Mr. President."

"PRESIDENT" BEFORE WASHINGTON

It should be interesting to note that, contrary to most history books, John Hanson of Maryland, not George Washington of Virginia, was actually the first President of the United States. The Continental Congress, operating under the Articles of Confederation—now called "Constitution I"—unanimously elected Hanson to a one-year term as "the first President of the United States in Congress assembled," in November, 1781, more than eight years before Washington assumed the Presidency under the now-existing Constitution, which has been dubbed "Constitution II."

WASHINGTON'S ASSISTANTS PROSPER

For the heads of the then-existing three government departments—State, Treasury, and War—Washington had only a few men to choose from. Benjamin Franklin, who was first looked upon as a candidate for Secretary of State, was finally rejected because at the age of 83 he was too old. So Washington—still attempting to appease the Democratic-Republicans—selected their leader, Thomas Jefferson, who was then America's ambassador to France.

Robert Morris, a Philadelphia banker, who was later severely criticized for the way in which he speculated in government securities to make large profits for himself, refused the job of Secretary of the Treasury and suggested Alexander Hamilton, a Federalist, which fell in nicely with Washington's plans for a strong central government.

General Henry Knox a friend of the President, who was named to fill the post of Secretary of War, did fairly well for himself financially by teaming up with Assistant Secretary of the Treasury William Duer in the promotion of the Scioto Company, which did a lot of wheeling and dealing in Ohio real estate. Duer, caught

WASHINGTON FOLLOWED HANSON of Maryland, and was not
the first President, as reported in many history books.

trading illegally in United States government bonds,
wound up in jail, much to Hamilton's embarrassment.

POLITICAL PATRONAGE BEGINS

Unfortunately, by confining most of his other appointments to members of the Federalist party, Washington not only gave the government its first powers of
patronage, but also made way for the "spoils system,"
by which the gainers of power could reward their friends
and punish their enemies by giving or taking away their
official jobs.

CABINET IN-FIGHTING BEGINS

No two men in Washington's Administration disagreed with each other more than Alexander Hamilton
and Thomas Jefferson. Hamilton, fighting against states'

rights, wanted to keep government power in one central place; Jefferson, fighting for states' rights, wanted to spread power around. Hamilton feared that trouble would result from too weak a central government; Jefferson feared that tyranny would result from too strong a central government. Hamilton wanted America to become an industrial nation; Jefferson wanted her to become an agricultural nation. Hamilton, who had been born in the West Indies, but, except as a child, had never lived outside of America, wanted her to be like Europe; Jefferson, who had lived outside of America, wanted her to be unlike Europe. Hamilton, fed up with the influence of Jeffersonians in government, quit his job as Secretary of the Treasury in 1794; Jefferson, fed up with the influence of Hamiltonians in government, and less tolerant than Hamilton, quit his job as Secretary of State in 1793, the first year of Washington's second term in office.

But, even with all of their differences, the two men had one thing in common: a love of sex. Hamilton, partly French in blood, was continually cheating on his wife, Elizabeth, and going to bed with Peggy Reynolds, the wife of a Philadelphia swindler; Jefferson, a widower at 39, was continually going to bed with Sally Hemings, one of his black slaves, who had five children by him.

THE INDIANS "PROTECTED"

The President and Congress, believing that the time had come to do something about the Indians, put through four laws that were supposed to improve the lives of the "first Americans": (1) The Indians' claims to their lands were to be guaranteed to them by the federal government, and they were to be allowed to govern themselves by their own tribal laws; (2) all Indian trade was to be federally regulated and controlled to

90

DRINKERS FOUGHT FOR WHISKY: Pennsylvanians, fighting for their "spirituous rights," refused to pay a whisky tax and beat up federal marshals who tried to collect it.

assure fair play in all business transactions; (3) white people were to be punished for abusing Indians, and Indians were to be punished for attacking whites; and (4) Indians living on their own lands were not to be taxed and were to be welcomed as American citizens, provided they were willing to settle among white people. But, as it so happened, few of these high-minded ideas, except exemption from taxation, were ever enforced or put into practice, owing to the weakness of the federal government and the greed of land-grabbers, such as Daniel Boone and Colonel George Rogers Clark. Washington himself broke the law when he decided, without consulting the Indians, to build a fort at Cincinnati, Ohio, in 1791.

WHISKY MOONSHINERS REBEL

A tax law, put through by the President and Congress in 1791 to collect taxes from distilleries, seemed as unjust and tyrannical to the people of the Appalachian Mountains, and beyond, as the British tax on tea had to all Americans in 1776. Distilling was about the only way to use surplus corn. Whisky could bear the high cost of transportation, and kegs of it were even used as money. Congress eased the law so that there would be less snooping by government agents. Opposition to the law quieted down, except in western Pennsylvania, where the whisky makers flatly refused to pay any tax. Led by Herman Husband and a frontier lawyer named David Bradford, the mountaineers terrorized law-abiding distilleries, beat up federal marshals at Pittsburgh, and called upon every citizen to rise and fight for his "spirituous rights." The revolt became jokingly known as the "Whisky Rebellion."

Thomas Mifflin, a member of the Democratic-Republican party and the governor of Pennsylvania, refused to enforce the tax law, fearful that it might cost him his popularity. Thereupon, President Washington, closely advised by Alexander Hamilton, decided to take action. A force of one thousand soldiers could have easily put down the insurrection. But Hamilton, anxious to show the power of the federal government over the state of Pennsylvania, had Washington call out 15,000 troops—an army almost as large as the one that won the American Revolution at Yorktown, Virginia, in 1781. The rebel leaders, noting the tremendous odds against them, fled, and the rank and file quit. The ringleaders, caught and tried for treason, were pardoned by the President. It was a serious but successful test of the power of the new government.

SUPPORT BRITAIN OR FRANCE?

Many Americans severely criticized the course that the Washington Administration took in foreign affairs. In 1793, when war began in Europe between Great Britain and France, Hamilton and his Federalist followers did their best to get America into the fight on the British side, fearing that unruly mobs with ideas of equality among men (the theme of the French Revolution of 1789) would bring a social revolution to the United States. Against them stood Jefferson and the Democratic-Republicans, who took sides with the French, chiefly because the British were illegally seizing American ships, and illegally using American real estate for trading posts in the Northwest Territory. Washington, aiming to keep America out of a foreign war, issued a proclamation proclaiming America's neutrality. He also sent John Jay, the first Chief Justice of the United States, to England to bring back for his signature a treaty, which made Britain give up a few of her Western trading posts, but recognized her claims in midwestern areas already settled by American families.

Taking advantage of the anger and discontent caused by all of this, Jefferson, along with James Madison, formed an alliance between unhappy Southern plantation owners and Western farmers, and gave new life to the Tammany Society, a political organization in New York City, which was headed by Aaron Burr, a clever politician, who had no use for Hamilton.

The Federalists held on to the Presidency in the election of 1796; their candidate, John Adams, barely beat Thomas Jefferson, who became Vice President. Adams knew politics, but was unfit, in Hamilton's opinion, for the "administration of government." He could not escape the shadow of the retired Washington and complained that he was not really President in his own right.

The retiring President was not unanimously applauded. The *Philadelphia Aurora*, on the day after Washington's retirement, proclaimed on its front page that "this day ought to be a Jubilee in the United States . . . for the man who is the source of all the misfortunes of our country . . . is this day reduced to a level with his fellow citizens." It was not a "lone voice" speaking in a vacuum.

93

15
ADAMS VERSUS JEFFERSON

John Adams, who played "hookey" for 385 days of his four years as President of the United States, managed to push through laws that worked not only to ruin his Administration, but also to violate the Constitution that he had sworn to protect when he took office on March 4, 1797.

One of these laws, aimed at weakening the Democratic-Republican party, did away with free speech and freedom of the press; another, aimed at increasing the power of the federal government, did away with states' rights. Democratic-Republican newspaper editors and others who saw fit to disagree with the President, criticize the government, or oppose the Federalist party were quickly silenced by heavy fines or lengthy jail sentences. Fearful that Adams was endangering personal and civil liberties and concentrating a dangerous power in the federal government, Thomas Jefferson and James Madison fought hard against these unjust laws, and finally got Congress to get rid of them in 1798–99. But it was not until 1801, when Jefferson became President, that the men whom Adams had sent to jail were freed from their cells.

PUBLIC PRESS

CONSTITUTION VIOLATED: Newspapers, deprived of the right of free speech, were not allowed to criticize the federal government.

JEWS WITHOUT RIGHTS

President Adams, supposedly a friend of the Jews, made no effort to help them in their battle for religious liberty, even though the Bill of Rights, added to the Constitution in 1791, had clearly guaranteed all Americans freedom of religion. Virginia refused to give Jews citizenship and banned them from testifying in court. Both Maryland and New Hampshire maintained a religious ban against Jews holding public office. Many years were to pass before the Jews of these three states were to be made full citizens.

"BENEFICIAL EXECUTIONS"

The President did nothing and said little about a serious slave rebellion that broke out in Virginia in the summer of 1800. The rebels, led by a slave known as "General" Gabriel, collected whatever rifles they could lay their hands on, and gathered for a march on the state capital at Richmond. Apparently they had hoped that a capture of key points in that city would trigger a

95

statewide revolt by cruelly treated slaves. But their plans were brought to a halt because two black "informers" warned government officials, and because a heavy rain made any action impossible.

The slaveholders were more than pleased by the way things turned out. No whites or blacks had been killed; but future safety called for some "beneficial executions." Within six weeks the affair was officially closed by the hanging of Gabriel and some 30 other blacks. Excited over the completion of the nation's new capital at Washington, D.C., most Americans gave little thought to the rebellion, and most newspapers gave little space to it. Although Gabriel and the men who died with him were all good Christians, no crosses were allowed on their graves.

DIRTY POLITICS

Presidential candidates for the election of 1800 were selected by party caucuses in Congress. The Democratic-Republican party, for states' rights and agriculture, nominated both Thomas Jefferson of Virginia and Aaron Burr of New York; the Federalist party, for a strong central government and industry, renominated John Adams of Massachusetts, with Charles Cotesworth Pinckney of South Carolina, as his running mate. The campaign was scurrilous, with dirty politics coming in to play. Jefferson was accused of being an atheist and a lover of the French; Adams was accused of being an autocrat and a lover of the British. There was talk of preventing an election, and of civil war. The threat of state militiamen being called in to maintain law and order quieted things down.

The Democratic-Republicans, helped by renegade Federalists, finally won. But, with Jefferson and Burr having tied for first place—due to the clumsy electoral system of that time—the election had to be thrown into

POLITICS LED TO KILLING: Aaron Burr, after losing the Presidential election, shot and killed Alexander Hamilton, who had prevented his winning the governorship of New York.

the House of Representatives. Until the 12th Amendment to the Constitution (1804) removed the possibility of a tie between two candidates on the same ticket, the House, voting by states, had to make the final choice, a majority of one state being necessary for election. Burr, disliked and mistrusted by a number of Congressmen, lost out in the voting, and Jefferson was elected President by a majority of two states. As prescribed by the system, Burr was made Vice President. Adams, pulling a fast one on his last day in office, found time to pack the new circuit and district courts with Federalist judges and to make John Marshall, an enemy of Jefferson, Chief Justice of the United States.

Actually, the election of 1800 brought about more changes in men than it did in government. Except for reducing the size of the Army and Navy and revising the federal court system, Jefferson left almost everything else as he had found it, including the mechanism for a strong central government. Although he had been quick to criticize anyone who violated the Constitution, the President himself "stretched the document till it cracked" in 1803, when he authorized the purchase of Louisiana from Napoleon's France for $15 million, without having first asked Congress to approve it, as he should have done. Many people accused him of "out-Federalizing the Federalists."

THE BIG DUEL

President Jefferson, not wanting the crafty Aaron Burr as his Vice President, dropped him in favor of George Clinton of New York in the election of 1804, which the Democratic-Republicans won hands down. Burr, out of a job, ran for governor of New York, but was undermined by Alexander Hamilton, who had no respect for him. Out for revenge, Burr challenged Hamilton to a duel on July 11, 1804. Hamilton, taking Burr's bullet in his chest, died 30 hours later.

BURR'S MONSTROUS PLAN

Andrew Jackson, a Tennessee politician and militia-man, who liked Aaron Burr, invited the "dueler" to move to his state and run for the Senate. But Burr had a much bigger idea in mind. Encouraged by his friend General James Wilkinson, the federal governor of the Louisiana Territory, he laid plans to raise money, organize an army, take Mexico from Spain and Louisiana from the United States, and set up a nation of his own. Wilkinson, considering the ex-Vice President's plan as "too dangerous," and deciding that he might be better off with one less friend, wrote President Jefferson toward the end of 1806, denouncing Burr as "deep, dark, and wicked." Within a very short time, Burr was caught and brought to Richmond, Virginia, for trial on the charge of treason against the United States. But Chief Justice John Marshall of the Supreme Court of the United States, performing his collateral role as a district-court judge, found a loophole in the law and

98

handed down a verdict of "not guilty," letting the defendant go free.

SUBPOENA OF THE PRESIDENT

Burr, out to do anything to win his case, had asked that President Jefferson be subpoenaed, and be made to produce certain letters that had been written to him by one of the witnesses for the prosecution. Chief Justice Marshall, dismissing the English idea that "the king can do no wrong," pointed out that the American Constitution held the President liable to impeachment and removal, and that he could be subpoenaed to appear as a witness. A more complicated issue was whether the President could be compelled to produce any document in his possession. Ruled Marshall: "The President, although subject to the general rules which apply to others, may have sufficient motives for declining to produce a particular paper . . . I can readily conceive that the President might receive a letter which it would be improper to exhibit in public, because of the manifest inconvenience of the exposure." Jefferson, well versed in law, handled the problem by denying that the Court had a right to subpoena his papers, and then went ahead and produced the letters anyhow. Thus the issue was never forced to a final test.

MADAME JUMEL'S BOAST

Regretting, no doubt, that he had not killed Jefferson instead of Hamilton, Burr took off for Europe, where he used his "charm" to obtain money for wild schemes that never amounted to anything. By some means, he got a passport and returned to the United States in 1812, built up a law practice in New York City, and, at 77, married Eliza Brown Jumel, a beautiful, red-headed wealthy widow, who boasted that she was the only woman in the world who had slept with both George

Washington and Napoleon Bonaparte. The mansion where she lived on New York City's Washington Heights is today a historic site, preserved by the city. Among the intriguing anecdotes in American history is the allegation that Martin Van Buren, the eighth President of the United States, was Burr's illegitimate son. John Quincy Adams's diary virtually says that it was true.

THE TRICKY MR. ASTOR

Jefferson, aiming to maintain America's neutrality and keep her out of the Napoleonic War that was raging in Europe, got Congress to pass the Embargo Act of 1807, which bottled up American ships in home ports so that they would avoid getting into any trouble with foreign men-of-war. But John Jacob Astor, who had branched out from trading in furs in the Oregon Country to trading with China, managed to get his ship *Beaver* out of America and back again by playing a trick on the President. A character, describing himself as "the Honorable Punqua Wingchong, a Chinese official," requested permission to charter a ship to return from New York to China, where his family affairs "particularly funeral rites of his grandfather, required his solemn attention."

Jefferson, thinking that this might serve to strengthen American relations with China, ordered Secretary of the Treasury Albert Gallatin, who knew Astor, to issue the necessary papers. Gallatin not only allowed the Honorable Punqua to sail with numerous "attendants" and $45,000 worth of merchandise, but also permitted the *Beaver* to bring a return cargo from China. As it all turned out, the Chinese official was nothing more than a clerk in Astor's employ, the cargoes were Astor's "speculations"; and the *Beaver*, returning to New York crammed with Chinese goods while the Embargo Act was still in effect, put her owner well on his way to becoming the richest man in America.

100

16
THE SECOND WAR
WITH ENGLAND

James Madison, described as "one of the chief architects of the Constitution," nearly proved to be the "undertaker" of the United States. Although he tried during his two terms in office (1809–17) to be as strong a President as Thomas Jefferson had been in his use of federal power, Madison went to war unnecessarily and fought it badly, and, by his mistakes, did much to hurt his country. Among the people at large, he inspired little affection and no enthusiasm. Unable to get along with Congress, he was often stubborn to the point of stupidity. Describing Madison, writer Washington Irving called him "but a withered little applejohn [dried-up apple]."

THE RISE OF THE WAR HAWKS

A group of young Congressmen, mainly from the South and West, quickly became fed up with President Madison's policy for keeping the peace, and loudly shouted for a war, believing that national honor demanded a fight. These men, collectively called the "War Hawks," got Congress to approve the raising of a regular army of 25,000 men, but did nothing to build a navy, contending that navies were evil.

Without getting anywhere, the members of the Federalist party argued that "if we must fight someone, we should fight France, since she has become the Number-One enemy to the free world, and an autocrat." But the War Hawks came up with a better reason for a fight with England.

War with Great Britain, if successful, would conquer Canada, end the Indian threat on the western frontier, and open up more land for settlement by American pioneers. John Randolph of Virginia, who led the old-fashioned Democratic-Republicans who wished to keep the peace, poured out his contempt for Congressman Henry Clay of Kentucky, the leader of the War Hawks, who boasted, "The conquest of Canada is in your power; the militiamen of Kentucky alone are competent to place Montreal and Upper Canada at your feet." For purely selfish reasons, this made sense to many Americans.

INDIANS GYPPED

Thomas Jefferson, aiming to establish western settlements and make America an agricultural nation, had taken land from the Indians, planning to make them move westward, beyond the Mississippi River. Such a policy could have been squared with humanity and justice by protecting the red men from the whites during the process, but Jefferson did not go that far. Although the Indians faithfully lived up to the agreements they had made with the federal government, the white pioneers in the Old Northwest—including Ohio, Indiana, Illinois, Michigan, Wisconsin, and the eastern part of Minnesota—murdered many red men, knowing that no pioneer jury would ever do anything about it. Hungry and poverty-stricken Indian chiefs, rounded up by government officials and plied with whisky, signed away the lands of their tribes without realizing what

102

INDIANS FOUGHT FOR RIGHTS: The Indians of the old Northwest, fed up with the bad treatment they were getting from the government, declared war against the United States in 1811.

they were doing. Jefferson had apparently seen nothing wrong with this sort of thing.

General William Henry Harrison, the superintendent of the Northwest Indians and governor of the Indian Territory, pushed the Indians so successfully that they parted with some 48 million acres of good land, between 1795 and 1809. Fed up with Harrison's land-grabbing and aiming to save his people, Tecumseh, the chief of the Shawnee Indians, declared war against the United States in 1811, but was put down by the general and one thousand soldiers in the Battle of Tippecanoe.

A CRY FOR A FIGHT

The white pioneers in the Old Northwest, believing that "British intrigue and British gold from Canadian mines" had encouraged the Indians to fight, now thought that "Canada must be conquered to insure the safety of the American frontier." The settlers in the Carolinas and Georgia went along with them, feeling that a war with England would enable them to take West Florida, which was then held by Spain, Britain's ally in her war with France. President Madison, stubbornly refusing to try and work things out with the British, who were seizing American ships and forcing American sailors into the British navy, gave in weakly to the War Hawks and asked Congress to declare war against Great Britain on June 18, 1812.

The war, according to historian Samuel Eliot Morison, was far from popular in America. Robert Smith, a former Secretary of State, and John Marshall, the Chief Justice of the United States, spoke out openly against Madison and the war, saying that Americans might as well be divided into two groups: one for the friends of peace and one for the advocates of war. The New England states, angered by their loss of foreign trade, refused to call out their militiamen for service in the Army of the United States, turned down the federal government's request to buy war bonds, and came close to leaving the Union. Maryland, a Democratic-Republican state, regretting its ever having supported the President in the first place, switched to the Federalist party. But, even with all of this going on, Madison was re-elected for another term in the election of 1812.

TORONTO AND WASHINGTON BURNED

The War Hawks got their wings painfully clipped by the war. After Captain Oliver Hazard Perry's victory over the British on the waters of Lake Erie, and an attempted invasion by American armed forces that resulted in the burning of government buildings in Toronto, the Army of the United States had to beat a hasty retreat. The British evened the score by burning much of Washington, D.C., while President Madison and members of Congress fled shamefully from the capital to hide in the woods. The huge distances over which the war was fought made any real victory unlikely. Neither side could effectively occupy the territory of the other.

ANTI-SEMITISM IN THE NAVY

Uriah Phillips Levy, who, at 20, quit his job as captain of a merchant ship to join the United States Navy in the War of 1812, was often embarrassingly snubbed or ignored by other officers, partly because he was a self-made skipper and not a graduate of Annapolis, and mostly because he was a Jew. Objecting to the cruel treatment that sailors were getting at sea and fighting anti-Jewish sentiment in the service, he wound up being court-martialed and downgraded in rank eight times during a period of 30-some years. Dropped by the Navy "without ceremony" in 1855, Levy continued to battle year in and year out for reinstatement. Finally, in 1860, one year before the War Between the States, he not only won his case, but was also elevated to the rank of commodore—the highest rank in the Navy at that time.

A POINTLESS BATTLE

The war, which brought about no great changes in the position of either side, was officially ended on December 14, 1814. But General Andrew Jackson, often described as "trigger-happy," continued it by fighting an unnecessary battle with the British at New Orleans, on January 8, 1815, claiming afterward that the news of the peace reached him too late.

The Midwest, largely vacated by the British, now became a choice location for the land-grabbing pioneers. The Indians, overpowered by the whites, were forced to move west of the Mississippi River. Even the Cherokees in Georgia, who had won court decisions in their favor, were driven off their lands.

SLAVE VERSUS FREE STATES

Slavery was by far the most serious of America's postwar problems. The North, which had been unhappy over the "federal arithmetic" that gave the South 20 seats and 20 votes in Congress, objected strongly to the admission of Missouri to the Union as a slave state, since it would give the Southerners more voting power. The South, not yet ready to defend the "rightfulness" of slavery, argued strongly that Missouri should be slave, not free. Both the North and the South threatened to leave the Union, and there was even talk of war. As a compromise, Maine, against slavery, was admitted to the Union at the same time, bringing about the balance of 12 free and 12 slave states.

But this action, arranged by Congressman Henry Clay and called the Missouri Compromise of 1820, did no more than put the question of slavery extension on ice. "This momentous question, like a fire bell in the night, awakened and filled me with terror," wrote Thomas Jefferson. "I considered it at once as the death knell of the Union."

THE "HANDS-OFF" DOCTRINE

A postwar idea of the next President, James Monroe, called the Monroe Doctrine, made it quite clear to European nations that America would not bother them if they did not bother her.

But John Jacob Astor, an American fur trader, who had become rich by offering Indians watered whisky in exchange for expensive furs, disregarded America's foreign policy and set up a trading post on British real estate in the Oregon Country. Fortunately, the British, who had agreed to share Oregon with the United States
106

at the end of the War of 1812, overlooked Astor's trespassing and kept the peace.

BANKING TROUBLES

The usual postwar depression, caused by too much
optimism and too much credit, began in 1819. The
Bank of the United States, a private financial institution
and the depository for the funds of the federal government, might well have put a brake on inflation at the
end of the war. But, no different from other banks, it
was eager to scramble for profits. The directors of the
bank, largely representing Eastern moneyed interests,
were far too slow to take steps to reduce credit. The 25
branches of the bank were ordered to cash in all state
bank notes immediately and to renew no personal loans
or mortgages. As a result of all of this, many state banks
were forced to close, and many owners of Western real
estate were forced to give up everything that they owned.

The Supreme Court, much to the surprise of many
people, handed down a startling decision, forbidding
states to tax the Bank of the United States. "All the
flourishing cities of the West are mortgaged to this money
power," declared Senator Thomas H. Benton of
Missouri. "They may be devoured by it at any
moment. They are in the jaws of the Monster. A lump
of butter in the mouth of a dog—one gulp, one swallow,
and all is gone."

17

ELECTIONS BY FOUL MEANS

The American people had become tired of being dictated to by the "Congressional caucus," which had been naming the candidates of the various parties in Presidential elections, and by the time the election of 1824 rolled around, the state legislatures were nominating their "favorite sons" for the Presidency. No member of the dying Federalist party chose to take part in this political campaign, and no advocate of states' rights yet ventured to come forward. All four of the final candidates—John Quincy Adams of Massachusetts, William Harris Crawford of Georgia, Henry Clay of Kentucky, and Andrew Jackson of Tennessee—were Democratic-Republicans, each representing a different faction of his party. But the real contest was between Adams, who reportedly favored the rich, and Jackson, who reportedly favored the poor. Jackson won more popular votes than Adams, but not enough to have a clear majority in the Electoral College. In keeping with the Constitution, the election went to the House of Representatives, which covered itself with disgrace.

WHEELING AND DEALING

The Congressmen, holding personal conferences in the barrooms and boardinghouses of the nation's capital, made a crafty deal by which Clay was to be given the job of Secretary of State, in return for his support of Adams. Satisfied with this arrangement, enough of the lawmakers voted for Adams in the House of Representatives to give him the necessary majority and the election. One of the publicized reasons for his victory was that, as the son of a former President, he would know much more about running the White House.

Clay, angered by what Senator John Randolph of Virginia said about Adams's having "bought" the Presidency, challenged the Virginian to a duel, but, fortunately, both statesmen were bad shots. Investigations of Presidential corruption were started but not finished, so that Adams had no chance to defend himself. With pro-Jackson Congressmen blocking everything that he tried to do in both domestic and foreign affairs, President Adams could well describe his term in office as "a harassing, wearying, teasing condition of existence."

DIRTY ELECTIONEERING

The Presidential election of 1828, with John Quincy Adams leading the newly formed National Republican party and Andrew Jackson leading the newly formed Democratic party, really smelled. Adams, who had furnished the White House at his own expense with a billiard table and a set of fancy chessmen, was accused by pro-Jackson newspapers of using public funds for "gaming tables and gambling furniture." One Jackson campaign speaker even went so far as to say that Adams was "playing pimp to the emperor of Russia." Jackson, described by pro-Adams newspapers as a "trigger-happy gunslinger," was said to have needlessly shot militiamen for insubordination while serving as a general in the War of 1812, and to have slept with his wife, Rachel, before they were married. The jackass, which oddly enough became the symbol of the Democratic party, was pictured on posters all over the country to make fun of Jackson's ignorance. Altogether, it was the most degrading election that the United States had ever experienced. More corrupt ones, however, were to come.

"THE PEOPLE'S CHOICE"

Jackson, "the people's choice," not only chalked up 56 per cent of the popular vote, carried the Southern and Western states, Pennsylvania, and most of New York, but also won 178 electoral votes to Adams's 83. Virginia, holding her aristocratic nose, voted for Jackson, seeing him as the "lesser of two evils"; South Carolina, voting for him as a "states' rights man," would soon realize that she had made a mistake. But, all things considered, it was classes rather than sections that elected Jackson. The hunters and backwoods farmers of the South saw him as "plain folk" like themselves; and the working class of the North liked what he said in his campaign about "equal rights for all, special privileges for none." In truth, however, Jackson cared little about the "common people" and had no use for blacks, whom he used as slaves, or Indians, whom he massacred.

THE MOB IN THE WHITE HOUSE

"Old Hickory," as Jackson had been nicknamed by the press, or "The Gineral," as he was called by his hillbilly friends, staged one of the wildest orgies ever to be held in Washington, D.C., on an Inauguration Day. The White House, with its doors wide open to the public, was nearly completely destroyed when some 20,000 Jackson admirers tried to force their way inside. Glasses were broken and crushed under foot, punch was spilled onto carpets, and upholstered furniture ruined by dirty
110

HILLBILLIES MOBBED THE WHITE HOUSE on Jackson's Inauguration Day, and came close to destroying it.

boots. Aristocrats shuddered over what they feared to be
the opening of a national rebellion. The pastor of the
capital's Unitarian church preached a sermon on
Luke xix. 41: "Jesus beheld the city and wept over it."

START OF THE SPOILS SYSTEM

Pro-Jackson newspaper editors and politicians, per-
sistently lying about the "extravagance and corruption"
of the Adams Administration, persuaded Jackson that
his first responsibility as President was to "cleanse the
stables of accumulated filth"; in other words, to fire
enough officeholders to make room for "deserving
Democrats." Rotation in office and the so-called "spoils
system" had long been popular in New York, Pennsylvania, and other Northern states. Many members of
the civil service had come out for Jackson, but others had
not.

Jackson, removing some 250 of Adams's appointees, remarked to a friend that he was "surprised at his own moderation." But small as it was, the "purge" caused much hardship, since there were then no pensions for aged or retired civil service employees. A few cases of crooked bookkeeping by earlier appointees were uncovered and reported by the press; but these were nothing compared to the scandals created by many of the men appointed by Jackson. One of them, a vote-getter by the name of Samuel Swartwout, managed to steal more than one million dollars in public money during the 10 years that he held the collectorship of the Port of New York.

A HUSSY UPSETS THE CABINET

A bit of whoring by Senator John H. Eaton of Tennessee and Mrs. Peggy O'Neale of Washington, D.C., not only upset the President, but also caused an uproar in the nation's capital. Mrs. O'Neale, the daughter of a tavernkeeper and wife of a navy officer, had become tired of lonely nights and sleeping alone, and invited Eaton to move in and share her bed. The Senator, not wishing to give up this pleasant arrangement, bought the tavern when Peggy's father went broke, and persuaded Secretary of the Navy John Branch to give her husband plenty of sea duty.

The seafaring husband, caught cheating the government out of money, either died or committed suicide (nobody knew which), and shortly after the news reached Washington on New Year's Day, 1829, his merry widow, now 32, announced her engagement to Eaton. Some friends of Eaton tried to break up the romance; but Jackson, aiming to prevent gossip and make Peggy an honest woman, practically commanded the Senator to arrange a hasty marriage, and, following the ceremony, appointed him Secretary of War. The

EATONS SUFFERED FOR THEIR PROMISCUITY: The Secretary of War and his wife were given the cold shoulder by Washingtonians, because they were known to have had premarital sex.

wife of Vice President John C. Calhoun refused to visit or entertain the "hussy," and the wives of other men in high places followed suit.

The crisis came at Jackson's birthday party on March 15, 1830, when the wives of the Secretaries of the Presidential Cabinet turned their backs on Peggy and insulted her. The President, observing all of this, called the Secretaries to a special meeting the very next day to discuss the "unjust treatment" of Mrs. Eaton, whom he described as a "woman of virtue." From that moment on, only the National Republicans questioned Peggy Eaton's morals.

ONE-MAN RULE

Andrew Jackson, who came up with his own brand of democracy, used Presidential power to the full during his two terms in office (1829–37). In 1832, when South Carolina declared that a new federal tax on imported goods was against the Constitution, and that she would leave the Union rather than pay it, the President quickly discouraged the revolt by threatening to use arms against the state. Against big business, Jackson destroyed the Bank of the United States by taking away its charter, and by removing all government deposits and putting the money in favored state banks. Chief Justice John Marshall handed down a decision giving the Cherokee Indians the right to keep their real estate in Georgia, but Jackson, who hated red men, defied the Court, and forced them to move west of the Mississippi River. Showing a contempt for Congress, he used the veto power of the Presidency more often than all of the previous Presidents put together, once declaring that he "would receive no message from the damned scoundrels in the Legislative branch."

In 1833, when Harvard decided to confer an honorary degree on Jackson and invited John Quincy Adams, a distinguished alumnus, to attend the ceremony, Adams declined the invitation and wrote Josiah Quincy, president of the university:

> As myself an affectionate child of our alma mater, I would not be present to witness her disgrace in conferring her highest literary honor upon a barbarian who could not write a sentence . . . and hardly spell his own name.

18

EXTENDING FREEDOM (AND SLAVERY)

Southern Congressmen, seeing the westward expansion of America as a possible means of maintaining a balance between free and slave states, were quick to support Democrat James Knox Polk of Tennessee, who promised to stretch the nation all the way to the Pacific Ocean when he became President in 1845. Polk, a man with a strong will, was to carry out what former President Andrew Jackson flatteringly described as "extending the area of freedom," and what many people enthusiastically praised as America's "manifest destiny." Polk's plan, which writer Harriet Martineau correctly called "the most high-handed theft of modern times," included not only the dividing of the Northwest with Great Britain, but also the taking of the Southwest from Mexico.

THE FIRST TEXANS

Mexico, eager for settlers, had invited cotton-growing Americans from the Southern states to set up housekeeping on her free Texas real estate in the 1820's, expecting them to obey Mexican laws, and particularly the one that banned slavery. But the immigrants, led by a greedy land-grabber named Stephen F. Austin, turned out to be a bunch of lawbreakers, and soon made a lot of trouble by refusing to pay taxes, free their slaves, or respect the Mexican army.

Things had become worse by the early 1830's, when the Texas settlers began to be outnumbered by a new breed of men—swashbucklers like Sam Houston, who had fought beside Andrew Jackson in the War of 1812 and against Indians; Branch T. Archer, who had fled from Virginia after killing a man in a duel; James Bowie, a slave smuggler, who had designed the long knife named after him; Davy Crockett, a professional backwoodsman; and others of restless ambition, who had left the United States for the country's good, and ended up in Texas.

The Texans, stirred up by the swashbucklers, decided to have it out with the Mexicans; and, after defeating the Mexican army in a bloody battle at San Jacinto in 1836, declared Texas an independent republic, legalized slavery, elected Sam Houston president, and sent a representative to Washington, D.C., to demand annexation to the United States or recognition as a nation. Houston, who had made up his mind that he would rather be a United States Senator than a Texas president, sold the Texans on annexation and looked to President Andrew Jackson to get the "Lone Star Republic" into the Union. Jackson, about to vacate the White House, passed the buck to his successor, Martin Van Buren, a professional Democratic politician from New York, who did little or nothing about it.

Texas, sorely tempted by this neglect to make some sort of deal with Great Britain or France, finally made it into the Union in 1845, when John Tyler of Virginia, a member of the new Whig party, described by historian Samuel Eliot Morison as a "good second-rate President," signed the necessary papers on his last day in office.

TEXANS ROBBED MEXICANS, taking just about everything they could get their hands on.

ROBBING THE MEXICANS

The Mexicans, feeling that they had already been sufficiently "robbed" by the Texans, came up with some strong arguments when the United States saw fit to extend the border of Texas southward from the Nueces River to the Rio Grande. President James Knox Polk responded by going to war with Mexico for two years (1846–48). At the war's end, the United States imposed a humiliating peace on the Mexican government by "buying" the Southwest from her at the point of a bayonet for a mere $15 million. A cheap price, indeed, for over 500,000 square miles of real estate, out of which were to come the states of California, Utah, Arizona, New Mexico, Nevada, and parts of Colorado and Wyoming.

Many intelligent Americans, regarding the Mexican War as a "conspiracy for more slave territory," fought strongly against it. Henry David Thoreau, a powerful social critic, refused to pay taxes and wrote his famous *Essay on Civil Disobedience* to justify himself. James Russell Lowell, a leading 19th-century poet, wrote in his *Biglow Papers:*

117

They just want this Californy
So's to lug new slave states in
To abuse ye, an' to scorn ye,
An' to plunder ye like sin.

The Legislature of Massachusetts declared it to be "a war to strengthen the slave power, a war against the Constitution and the free states, insupportable by honest men, to be concluded without delay, and to be followed by all constitutional efforts for the abolition of slavery within the United States." But that was all talk. Even the Northern "conscience Whigs," as the antislavery wing of the political party was called, flinched before actually obstructing the war.

DIVIDING OREGON

Fortunately, the dividing of the Northwest (Oregon Country) between the Americans and the British was carried out without any bloodshed and required nothing more than a little arithmetic. The United States got all of the real estate south of what is now the Canadian border, while Great Britain got what is now British Columbia. Except for a few minor arguments over the islands of Puget Sound, the sharing of this western end of the lengthy frontier between Canada and the United States caused no other trouble.

But even with America straddling the continent, President Polk was still not satisfied. Hopeful of making the Gulf of Mexico an American lake, he did his best to take Cuba from Spain and Nicaragua from herself. His luck must have changed. Neither of these land-grabbing schemes materialized.

With her attention necessarily turned inward by the problems of slavery and the threat of civil war, America could make no further attacks on other nations for 50 years.

19

A BIT OF HORSE TRADING

The Southern states, angered over the prospect of California's entering the Union as a free state and the North's gaining the balance of power in the Senate, came close to separating themselves from the United States in 1850. Indeed, they might have seceded right then and there if Senator Henry Clay of Kentucky had not indulged in a bit of horse trading and come forward with another compromise. His plan, calling for each side to take a little and give a little, satisfied the South by leaving other recently acquired Mexican real estate open to slavery, and satisfied the North by acknowledging California as a free state. In addition, it also provided for a new fugitive slave law, requiring Northerners to return runaway slaves to slaveholders, which pleased the South; and abolished the slave trade in Washington, D.C., which pleased the North. Thus Senator Clay's Compromise of 1850 kept the Union together, temporarily at least.

"BLEEDING KANSAS"

Another compromise, the Kansas-Nebraska Act of 1854, set aside the Missouri Compromise of 1820, which had banned slavery anywhere north of the

119

border of that state. Pushed through Congress by Senator Stephen A. Douglas of Illinois, a heavy speculator in Western real estate, the new Act admitted Kansas and Nebraska from the Louisiana Purchase as territories, and turned over the question of slavery to local squatters. Senator Sam Houston of Texas reminded the Senate that most of Kansas and Nebraska legally belonged to the Indians. But who cared about the redskins? Government agents bullied them into giving up their real estate.

Thousands of slaveholders now moved into Kansas, and voted in a pro-slavery government, only to be attacked by gangs of Northern antislavers, led by fanatics such as the half-crazed John Brown. Open warfare broke out in "Bleeding Kansas," and terror was used by slavers and antislavers alike. Douglas, no longer considered "the idol of Northern democracy," reported that he "could travel from Boston to Chicago by the light of his burning effigies."

"The passing of the Kansas-Nebraska Act makes the fugitive slave law a dead letter throughout New England," wrote a Southerner who was visiting in Boston. "As easily could a law prohibiting the eating of codfish and pumpkin pie be enforced." On May 26, 1854, the day after the Act was signed by President Franklin Pierce, the federal government called out the Army in Boston and spent some $40,000 to return Anthony Burns, a fugitive slave, to his Southern master. He was the last to be returned from Massachusetts.

REPUBLICANS REGENERATED

The slavery issue gave rise to a new political group with an old name, the Republican party. Originally a "party of moral ideas," it never quite lost all of the reformers within its ranks, even when big business later dominated the party. Above all, the Republicans had one moral idea about the Union, summed up by Abraham Lincoln shortly before the War Between the States: "It will become all one thing, or all the other. Either the opponents of slavery will arrest the further spread of it, and place it where the public mind shall rest in the belief that it is in the course of ultimate extinction; or its *advocates* will push it forward, till it shall become alike lawful in *all* the states, *old* as well as *new—North* as well as *South.*"

THE KNOW-NOTHINGS

The Know-Nothings, another new political party, made up of anti-foreign and anti-Catholic flag wavers, became convinced that America was in danger from the Pope in Rome, and decided to do something about it. The party, which got its name from members, who, when questioned about their political activities, answered, "I know nothing." Later on, it got nowhere in the Presidential election of 1856, when it lured ex-President Millard Fillmore of New York away from the Whig party and picked him as its nominee for the Presidency.

But other Know-Nothing candidates for public office, well supported by their Protestant followers, developed surprising strength, and many small-time professional politicians joined up, thinking that this was the "party of the future." In state elections of 1854, the Know-Nothings had almost won New York, and did win in Massachusetts, electing a Legislature that conducted outlandish investigations of foreigners and the heads of Catholic schools and convents. In Baltimore, they organized gangs to beat up voters who refused to buy their way of thinking. In St. Louis, there were pitched battles between Protestants and Catholics. Police and militiamen were helpless, eight lives were lost, and order was restored only after Mayor Edward Bates organized some 800 armed citizens to put down the raving mobs. Later, the Know-Nothings became known as the American party, but even with the new name, the entire movement gradually fell apart.

INTERFERING AMERICANS

The "Young Americans," organized by younger members of the Democratic party in the 1840's to promote patriotism and spread the idea of democracy overseas, talked wildly about taking over Ireland and Sicily, as certain rebel leaders in those countries had suggested; and when newspapers announced that Hungary had fallen before a Russian army and had been forcibly made a part of Austria, the Legislatures of New York, Ohio, and Indiana called for action, demanding that the United States do something to help the conquered nation.

Daniel Webster of Massachusetts, serving as President Millard Fillmore's Secretary of State, insulted the emperor of Austria by writing him: "The power of this republic [the United States] at the present moment is spread over a region, one of the richest and most fertile on the globe, and of an extent in comparison with which the possessions of the House of Hapsburg are but as a patch on the earth's surface."

Louis Kossuth, a Hungarian leader, who had been invited to visit New York City as a guest of the United States in 1851, was shocked at hearing Senator Stephen A. Douglas say, "Europe is antiquated, decrepit, and tottering on the verge of dissolution. It is a vast graveyard."

NICARAGUAN CAPERS

An incident at San Juan del Norte (Greytown), Nicaragua, might well have triggered off a war between the United States and Great Britain in 1854. Solon

AMERICA COURTED TROUBLE: The U.S.S. Cyane came close to involving the United States in a war with England, by destroying British property during the course of a Nicaraguan brawl.

Borland, the United States ambassador to the Central-American nation, got himself involved in a local political brawl and was hit on the head with a bottle. Angered by what had happened and convinced that America had been insulted, he wrote President Franklin Pierce, urging him to do "whatever was necessary." The President responded by ordering the *U.S.S. Cyane* to the scene to demand an apology from the government; and, when none was forthcoming, her commander bombarded the town, destroying some British real estate during the action. The British government asked for compensation and got nothing; the British press blustered and threatened war, but by this time England was too busy fighting in the Crimea, and let the matter drop.

"Commodore" Cornelius Vanderbilt, the owner of a fleet of ships and a railway that carried both passengers and freight between New York City and Albany, New York, decided to add to his already large bank account by setting up a steamboat and stagecoach company in Nicaragua to compete with the Panama Railway. Quick to see that a lot more money could be made by taking over the government of the weak and troubled country, the Commodore hired William Walker, a notorious adventurer, who, by some means or another, managed to become president of Nicaragua.

Walker, "the gray-eyed man of destiny," as his

friends called him, became overly ambitious and was about to try to conquer the rest of Central America, when he made the big mistake of getting into a hot argument over money with the cagey Vanderbilt. The Commodore, who took no rough talk from any man, fired the president on the spot and gave his full support to a Central-American coalition that invaded Nicaragua and gained control of the nation. Walker, encouraged largely by Jefferson Davis, President Pierce's Secretary of War, made two more tries at becoming a Central-American president, and finally met his death in front of a Honduran firing squad.

The Latins, unable to forget the *U.S.S. Cyane's* bombardment and Walker's ambition, remained suspicious of, and hostile to, the United States for many a long year.

20
ON THE ROAD TO WAR

Was there a way to prevent the North and the South from having a head-on collision? The antislavers, with all of their talk and public demonstrations, were of no help. William Lloyd Garrison, a New England reformer and abolitionist, who had denounced the Constitution as "a covenant with death and an agreement with hell," publicly burned a copy of the document to dramatize this odd theory. But this meant little or nothing. There was but one proposal that made any sense, and that came from Ralph Waldo Emerson, a Massachusetts essayist and poet, who, speaking before the Anti-Slavery Society of New York, proposed that funds be raised to buy and free the slaves from their owners. "The federal government and the states could give the proceeds from the sale of public lands. . . . The churches will melt their [gold] plate . . . wealthy benefactors will give their thousands, and school children their pennies . . . every man in the land would give a week's work to dig away this accursed mountain of sorrow once and forever out of the world."

Nobody bought his idea. The Southerners refused to give up slavery, and the Northerners refused to pay them to do it. Emerson's estimated cost of $2 billion for carrying out the plan would have been cheap enough in comparison with that of the War Between the States, which was now threatening to take place.

BRUTALITY IN THE SENATE

Senator Charles Sumner of Massachusetts, a leading antislaver, delivered a hotly worded speech before Congress on May 19, 1856, during which he described Senator Andrcw Pickens Butler of South Carolina as "a Don Quixote whose Dulcinea was the harlot of slavery," and Senator Stephen A. Douglas as "Sancho Panza, the squire of slavery, ready to do its humiliating offices." The speech, as described by the press, was so nasty that it would have probably ended Sumner's political career, had not "Southern chivalry" demanded physical punishment. Three days after it was made, Congressman P. S. Brooks, a cousin of Butler, beat Sumner senseless with a heavy stick while he was sitting helplessly in the Senate. The assailant was not only highly praised by Southern newspapers for his "gallantry," but was also presented with a "suitably engraved" walking cane. Sumner, badly injured, was forced to spend most of his time at home for the next three years; but he was now loudly praised as a hero in the North.

A PRO-SLAVERY PRESIDENT

James Buchanan, a Pennsylvania Democrat and Southern sympathizer, who had long had his eye on the White House, was now about to realize his ambition. The "Black Republicans," as the Democrats called them, picked as Buchanan's opponent John Charles Frémont of California, who had gained fame exploring the West, and had served as an officer in the Mexican War. "Free soil, free speech, and Frémont" was their slogan.

Southern leaders, ready to do anything to keep

SENATOR SUMNER OF MASSACHUSETTS TOOK A BEATING
from Congressman Brooks of South Carolina, for having verbally
attacked the Southerner's cousin in Congress.

Frémont out of the White House, warned the nation
that the South would secede from the Union if he were
elected President. When John M. Botts, a Virginia
statesman and anti-secessionist, called this an idle
threat, the *Richmond Enquirer* advised him to leave the
state "lest he provoke the disgrace of lynching."
Buchanan carried every slave state except Maryland—
together with Pennsylvania, Illinois, and Indiana—and
won with 174 electoral votes to Frémont's 114. He was
the first bachelor to be elected President of the United
States.

The newly elected President had looked forward to a
peaceful term in office, but before his Administration
was one week old, newspapers across the nation carried
the story of one of the most sensational trials in American
history, up to that time.

ARE BLACKS "PROPERTY"?

Dred Scott, a slave, who had been taken by his master from the slave state of Missouri to the free territory of Minnesota, and then back to Missouri, decided to sue for his freedom, basing his argument on the fact that he had resided on free soil. Antislavers claimed that he was a free man; slavers claimed that he was still a slave.

The case, considered as highly controversial, reached the Supreme Court of the United States, where Chief Justice Roger Brooke Taney, along with four Associate Justices, all from the South, saw it as an opportunity to settle the question of slavery in the territories by extending it legally to all parts of the nation. President-elect Buchanan, anxious to make the Democrats happy, had put the Justices up to it, and two of them tipped him off on the decision in advance, so that he could include the "good news" in his inaugural address.

The Court, which published its decision two days after Buchanan was sworn into office on March 4, 1857, decided against Scott's claim for freedom. As Chief Justice Taney pointed out, a black could not be a citizen of the United States, and therefore had no right to sue in a federal court. A slave was "property," and property could be taken anywhere. Congress could not take away any man's property and could not pass laws to end slavery or to limit the areas in which it could exist. Any laws that it had passed to limit slavery were not allowed by the Constitution. Dred Scott was still a slave.

COURT AND CONSTITUTION CRITICIZED

Attacking both the Court and the Constitution, William Cullen Bryant, a poet and editor of the *New York Evening Post*, wrote: "Hereafter, if this decision shall stand for law, slavery, instead of being what the people of the slave states have hitherto called it, their peculiar institution, is a federal institution, the common patrimony and shame of all the states, those which flaunt the title of free, as well as those which accept the stigma of being the Land of Bondage; hereafter, wherever our jurisdiction extends, it carries with it the chain and the scourge—wherever our flag floats, it is the flag of slavery. If so, that flag should have the light of the stars and the streaks of morning red erased from it; it should be dyed black, and its device should be the whip and the fetter. Are we to accept, without question, these new readings of the Constitution . . .? Never! Never!"

The splitting up of the Democratic party, caused by arguments over slavery, and the refusal of traditional politicians to accept a government at the hands of the recently organized Republican party led directly to the War Between the States. Abraham Lincoln, a gangling and relatively unknown office seeker from Illinois, captured the Republican nomination and won the Presidential election of 1860. A little over a month after he moved into the White House, the North and the South were at war.

21
A NATION UNDER TWO FLAGS

Abraham Lincoln, whose policy, at the beginning, called for preserving the Union rather than freeing the slave, wielded a greater power throughout the War Between the States than any other President of the United States prior to Franklin D. Roosevelt. According to historian Samuel Eliot Morison, the Illinois Republican was not only a tyrant, but also a "dictator from the standpoint of American constitutional law." As Commander-in-Chief of the Army and Navy, he saw fit to call for enlistments without the approval of Congress, and to suspend the writ of *habeas corpus* (an order requiring that a prisoner be brought before a judge or into a court to decide whether he is being held lawfully).

Simultaneously with the Emancipation Proclamation of January 1, 1863, Lincoln issued an order that seemed to deny white citizens the liberty that he proposed to give black slaves. According to this order, all persons resisting the draft, discouraging enlistment, or "guilty of any disloyal practice affording comfort to rebels" would be subject to martial law, tried by the military, and denied the writ of *habeas corpus*. A national defense act, passed by Congress and signed by the President, contained a sentence that kept Jewish servicemen from having Jewish chaplains. It was not until 1862, when daily newspapers in New York City, Philadelphia, and Baltimore supported Judaism's right to representation, that the law was finally changed.

A DISLIKE FOR BLACKS

Although the North was presumably fighting to free the slaves, many Northern leaders despised blacks, and showed it. Their attitude toward blacks was not only ambiguous and inconsistent, but even hypocritical, revealing that Northerners, no less than Southerners, disliked any sort of relationship with colored people that would suggest equality. Many free blacks in the North, along with slaves who had escaped from the South, were used by the Union Army as labor troops, but most of the runaways in the South were simply kept alive in Union concentration camps. Blacks in the North were not allowed to fight for their own freedom until 1863, when Lincoln issued the Emancipation Proclamation. Yet, in Boston, from which the first black regiments departed to do battle in the South, there is an inscription on St. Gaudens's monument which reads: "Together they gave . . . undying proof that Americans of African descent possess the pride, courage, and devotion of the patriot soldier."

NORTHERN DRAFT DODGERS

The draft law, passed by Congress in 1863, favored the rich, and not the poor that Lincoln seemingly cared so much about. Wealthy young Northerners such as John D. Rockefeller, James Mellon, William Vanderbilt, and others who had a distaste for gunpowder had the choice of either hiring substitutes to fight for them or of buying an exemption by the payment of $300 to the government. No one of them ever wore a uniform.

The working class saw the system as highly unfair, and

131

**FIRST RECRUIT CO.
DRAFT EXEMPTION $300**

RICH ESCAPED DRAFT: Wealthy men who did not want to go to war were allowed to hire substitutes, or "buy" their way out of it.

when the first drawing of names for military service took place, there were bloody riots in a number of Northern cities. Archbishop John Hughes, who later visited Europe to argue the Union cause with Catholic leaders, warned Edwin M. Stanton, Lincoln's Secretary of War, that Roman Catholics were "willing to fight to the death for the support of the Constitution, the government, and the laws of the country, but not for the abolition of slavery." The hatred of Irish-Americans for blacks, as described by Morison, broke out viciously in New York City, where former slaves had been brought in to break a stevedores' strike. Rioters took over the city for four days and nights, destroying shops and homes of anti-slavers, gutting saloons, and lynching and torturing blacks. Troops had to be called in to restore order and quiet things down.

DISSENSION IN THE CONFEDERACY

Jefferson Davis, a Mississippi Democrat, who was elected president of the newly formed Confederate States of America in 1861, did not get along too well with his vice president, Alexander H. Stephens, who once said that "the foundations of slavery are laid . . . upon the great truth that the Negro is not equal to the white man; that slavery . . . is his natural and moral condition." Stephens, who hated Davis as much as he hated the War Between the States, was away from his job for 18 months during his four years in office. Linton Stephens, the vice president's brother, made no bones about carrying on a sniping campaign against Davis, whom he described as "a little conceited, hypocritical, sniveling, canting, malicious, ambitious, dogged knave and fool."

Governor Joseph E. Brown of Georgia, who was very much against the Confederate draft law, brought his state close to a point of revolt by 1864. Confederate congressman Robert Barnwell Rhett of South Carolina, the first state to leave the Union in 1861, even went so far as to plan a convention of Southern states to get Davis thrown out of office. Governor Zebulon B. Vance of North Carolina, another sharp thorn in Davis's side, did his best to keep for his state all of the uniforms that were made by North Carolinians, and to take the pick of all of the supplies that Southerners managed to get by the Union warships that were blockading the Confederate coastline.

The Confederate draft law exempted conscientious objectors, railway employees, teachers, clergymen, and the like. Later, the Confederate congress lengthened the list of "exempts" by including newspaper editors, printers, and plantation supervisors at the rate of one to every 20 slaves, which was loudly criticized by the poor whites. The hiring of substitutes, as in the North, was allowed until the end of 1863, when President Davis was forced to abolish the system and cut down on all exemptions.

The Confederacy, seeing the use of blacks in military

service as a "crowning indignity," used them largely as cooks, officers' servants, laborers, and teamsters, sometimes allowing them to enlist in the army and draw army pay. The blacks who wished to bear arms for the South had to wait until just before General Robert E. Lee's Confederate Army surrendered to General Ulysses S. Grant's Union Army at Appomattox, Virginia, in 1865, before they were even considered as fighting men. Surprisingly enough, they had been willing to serve without any promise of emancipation.

NORTHERN ARISTOCRATS AND PROFITEERS

Life in the North was pretty much the same in war as in peace. There were dinner, card, and theatre parties, as well as dances and other social functions in the cities in winter, and horse racing, boating, gambling, and swimming on Long Island and at Saratoga Springs in summer. P. T. Barnum, the owner of a circus that was billed as "The Greatest Show on Earth," staged one of his most successful productions in New York City on February 10, 1863, when "General" Tom Thumb, his two-foot-five-inch midget, married the equally tiny Mercy Lavinia Bump. The circus-goers, wearing formal attire and riding in glittering carriages, were described by the *New York Times* as "the elite, the crême de la crême, the bonton, the select few, the very First Families of the City, nay of the Country."

Northern industry, much to the surprise of the Confederacy, not only survived without its Southern market, but also grew and prospered. The government, generously handing out war contracts and lavishly spending taxpayers' money, made way for a new aristocracy of profiteers, who became notorious capitalists after the War Between the States. Because of the relatively slow advancement of labor unions, earnings did not match living costs. Average prices rose 117 per

134

cent, while average wages rose only 43 per cent between 1860 and 1865.

Wide speculation went on in goods and produce of all sorts. In Cleveland, the young merchant John D. Rockefeller prospered with the rising prices of food, earning upward of $17,000 a year (a fabulous income in those days). In Chicago, Philip D. Armour, the owner of a meat-packing business, supplied tons of salt pork and dressed beef, both for the Union Army and export. Even William, the slow-witted son of "Commodore" Cornelius Vanderbilt, sold hay from his Staten Island farm to the cavalry troops that were quartered nearby. James Mellon, the son of a millionaire Pittsburgh banker, pleaded with his father to put up money for speculation. "People are making millions in wheat," he reported from Wisconsin. "They continue to grow richer and don't care when the war ends."

Jay Cooke, a Philadelphia banker, "loaned" a great deal of money to Salmon P. Chase, Lincoln's Secretary of the Treasury, who showed his gratitude to the Philadelphian by granting him almost a complete monopoly in handling the sale of government war bonds. A good salesman, Cooke earned some $3 million a year in commissions by selling them at the rate of $2 million a day to "armchair patriots" and investors, whose only interest in the war was making money out of it. Congress, feeling that the government owed much to Cooke for the good work that he was doing, gave him a franchise to operate a horsecar line in the nation's capital. Chase, hopeful of becoming Chief Justice of the United States, got the job when Lincoln won a second term in the Presidential election of 1864.

Simon Stevens, a gun dealer, and J. P. Morgan, a New York City banker and financier, saw a way of reaping a nice profit for themselves by buying 5,000 defective rifles from a government warehouse and selling

CORRUPT SUPPLIERS SUPPLIED FAULTY RIFLES and other shoddy items to the Union Army, putting profit ahead of patriotism.

them to the Union Army. The rifles, which were delivered in due course to General John C. Frémont's army in the West, blew off the thumbs of the soldiers who fired them. A Congressional committee, investigating the whole affair, unearthed the startling fact that the government, in one day, had actually sold for $17,486 rifles which it had agreed the day before to purchase for $109,912. Both Stevens and Morgan were called to Washington, D.C., and charged with fraud and extortion. But, as things turned out, they both got off scot-free. Some historians have disputed these allegations, or given them no credence.

Cornelius Vanderbilt, who now controlled both steamship lines and railroads, did his "patriotic duty" by serving as a shipping consultant to the War Department, which gave him full authority to buy or lease ships for the transporting of troops from the North to the South. Not wishing to spend too much time away from his moneymaking operations in New York City, Vanderbilt worked largely through an agent, who collected a purchasing commission of five to 10 per cent while paying what were later thought to be high rentals of $800 to $900 a day for worn-out lake and river steamers. The most serious charge leveled against Vanderbilt, afterward, was that he had bought the ancient lake steamship *Niagara* for $10,000, knowing full well that it was to be used to carry Union troops from Northern cities to New Orleans. The ship, unfit for ocean travel, miraculously encountered no storms and safely reached its destination. A Congressional investigation, prompted by letters received from soldiers who had worried about their lives during the voyage, revealed that most of the beams of the *Niagara* did not have the "slightest capacity to hold a nail."

But with General Grant's complaining daily about shoddy blankets, doctored-up horses, useless rifles, sickening beef, and lousy railroad service, Vanderbilt's faults were largely overlooked. Historian Gustavus Myers, in his account, held that Vanderbilt "split" all commissions with his agent, a procedure that was perhaps not unusual.

In the general jubilation at the end of the war, Vanderbilt was among those who were awarded medals by Congress, in recognition of their "patriotism and loyal services."

SOUTHERN SOCIETY

The Confederate States of America, fighting for independence and race supremacy, saw the war as the only business of the day. Southerners, on the whole, gave their government more, and asked for less, than Northerners did. Southern women, left alone to run plantations, had to direct the necessary change from cotton-growing to food production, revive household industries, such as weaving and dyeing cloth, feed passing armies, and care for wounded Confederates.

But in Richmond, the capital of the Confederacy, society, for the most part, remained gay and hospitable, despite high prices. "You can always buy an egg for a dollar," wrote the editor of the *Examiner*. Baron von Borcke, a volunteer on General J.E.B. Stuart's staff, promoted formal balls, during which Southern debutantes were introduced. Henry R. Vizetelly, a war correspondent for the *Illustrated London News,* helped the women to plan parties and theatricals. Meanwhile, financial speculators, wearing the finest of clothes and drinking the best of wines, offered as great a contrast to the South's working class as the profiteers in Northern cities did to the North's working class.

AMERICA SEEN AS OBNOXIOUS

It is not too surprising that the United States had few true British, Canadian, and French friends in the years 1861–65. Opinions divided ideologically: the restoration of the Union would mean a victory for democracy; the destruction of the Union, a disaster for democracy.

America had long been obnoxious to the ruling classes of Europe and Canada, for the encouragement that she gave to liberal and radical groups. Wrote the Comte de Montalembert, a French statesman and writer: "An all-powerful and unconquerable instinct at once arrayed on the side of the proslavery people all the open or secret partisans of the fanaticism and absolutism of Europe."

Many European liberals, however, could see no difference between the Confederacy's struggle for independence and the nationalist movements in Ireland and other parts of Europe, which they had supported. European humanitarians, favoring a war against slavery, were constantly confused by the declarations of Lincoln to the effect that "slavery was not an issue." Exporters noted with no small measure of interest the Union's favoring of high taxes on imported goods, which the Confederacy loudly criticized. Shipping interests hoped for the defeat of the North, their toughest competitor, and looked forward to a new "cotton kingdom" in the South, for which they could handle the carrying trade.

But luck was on the side of the Union. Some 22,500,000 people and all of the means of war production stood behind Lincoln. The Confederate

States of America, with only 5,500,000 whites and 3,500,000 slaves, was pitifully short of industry and had to import many war necessities. The North was also able to raise twice the number of men and twice the amount of real money available to the South. Both armies took a great amount of punishment. One American out of every 50 lost his life.

Abominable as the institution of slavery was, to fight a great war over it and then to resinstate it in other forms was worse. And for the nation, a century later, to refuse the black people's demands for citizenship and fair play when their patience finally ran out—and after they had again and again proved the merits of their case in the highest court of the land over the better part of two decades—was to endorse injustice on a national scale.

22

IMPEACHMENT AND RECONSTRUCTION

Andrew Johnson, a "pro-Lincoln Democrat" from Tennessee, who moved up from the Vice Presidency to the Presidency when Abraham Lincoln was killed by an assassin's bullet, was the first Chief Executive ever to be faced with impeachment. In short, it was one of the most disgraceful episodes in American history.

The Radical leaders of the Republican party, angered by Johnson's refusal to go along with their ideas for the reconstruction of the Union, aimed at capturing the federal government and putting a muzzle on Presidential authority. As they wanted it, Congress would be the final judge of its own powers; and the President, along with his Cabinet, would be wholly responsible to the legislators. The opening move of the game, the Tenure of Office Act of 1867, made it impossible for the President to control his Administration, by requiring him to obtain the advice and consent of the Senate in the hiring and firing of government officials.

President Johnson, convinced that the Tenure of Office Act was contrary to the Constitution, decided to test it by dismissing Secretary of War Edwin M. Stanton, who had long been working hand in hand with the Radicals in Congress, and obstructing everything that he tried to do. The Secretary refused to leave and barricaded himself in the War Department. A little over six months later, on February 24, 1868, the House of Representatives impeached the President before the Senate, "for high crimes and misdemeanors," with Chief Justice Salmon P. Chase presiding.

Benjamin F. Butler of Massachusetts and Thaddeus Stevens of Pennsylvania, who led the committee appointed by the House of Representatives to prosecute Johnson, appealed to every prejudice and passion, and rode roughshod over every legal obstacle in their ruthless attempt to convict the President. At one point, they even went so far as to spread the rumor that Johnson had been an accessory to the murder of Lincoln.

But William M. Evarts, a leading American lawyer and statesman, and Benjamin R. Curtis, a former Associate Justice of the Supreme Court, who defended the President, tore the prosecution's case to pieces. There were no valid reasons, legal or otherwise, for impeachment. Yet, the Radicals came within one vote of ejecting Johnson from the White House. Only the courage of a few independent Republican Senators like Lyman Trumbull of Illinois, James W. Grimes of Iowa, and William Pitt Fessenden of Maine, who were willing to sacrifice their political future by voting for acquittal, saved him. Stanton, who resigned from his job as Secretary of War at the end of the trial, was appointed as an Associate Justice of the Supreme Court when Ulysses S. Grant took over the White House in 1869, but died before he could take his seat.

THE FIGHTING IRISH

The Irish Revolutionary Brotherhood of New York City, better known as the Fenians, decided to invade Canada in the spring of 1866, and hold her as hostage until Ireland gained her independence from Great

Britain. Dressed in glittering uniforms of green and gold and armed with rifles, the Irishmen headed north with the intention of taking over the Canadian island of Campobello (later, the summer home of Franklin D. Roosevelt), but were stopped dead in their tracks by federal officials at Eastport, Maine. The ensuing howl from Irish voters, with Congressional elections only six months away, scared the living daylights out of President Andrew Johnson and members of his Cabinet —and before they could decide who should take the blame for stopping him, "General" John O'Mahony ferried 1,500 troops across the Niagara River and raised the flag of Ireland over old Fort Erie. The next day, the Canadian militia gave battle and fled; but the Fenians, too, fled back to New York, where they were arrested and promptly set free. Ridiculous and futile as their efforts were, the Fenians caused Canada much trouble and expense, for which she was never reimbursed by the United States. Anglo-American tension increased substantially.

PROFITEERING IN LAND

The United States, disunited by the War Between the States, was in sorry need of reconstruction in 1865. High tariffs on imports had made way for the rapid growth of Northern industries and helped to pay for the war; but inflation had halved the value of the dollar, while profiteering had created millionaires without spreading the wealth. The millionaires rapidly corrupted the Republicans whose party became the party of big business and high tariffs, while the poor were made to pay more for imported goods and almost everything else that they purchased.

The Homestead Act, which had been put through by Congress and signed by Abraham Lincoln in 1862, may have given 160 acres of free Western land to anyone who
142

would farm it for five years, but it also encouraged speculators to take over government lands by using "dummy settlers" to get title to large pieces of real estate after only six months of occupation at the low fixed price of $1.25 an acre. Another 131,350,000 acres went for nothing to the Southern Pacific, Northern Pacific, Union Pacific, and Sante Fe Railroads, all of which were largely controlled by Eastern capitalists, who, with the help of friends in Congress, made millions of dollars from the coal, copper, oil, gold, and silver that they discovered on their property.

"PORK-BARREL" POLITICS

The Radical Republicans reconstructed little during Reconstruction. They left the West to the mercy of the Eastern moneymakers, whom they failed to hold in check. They inflicted an offensive, corrupt government on the defeated South and made it a poverty area for many years to come. It was true that the South took advantage of Andrew Johnson's leniency to put prewar leaders back in power, and to pass laws that served to reduce freed blacks to a condition bordering on slavery; but none of these laws justified the brutal counterattack of the Radicals.

Johnson, who stupidly attempted to fight Congress rather than to compromise with it, vetoed bills for the continuance of the Republican "pork barrel" and political machine in the South; for the Freedmen's Bureau, which provided relief work and education for blacks and poor whites; and for civil rights. Congress responded by imposing military rule on the Southern states, and by pushing through the 14th Amendment to the Constitution, which gave blacks their American citizenship and protected their civil rights; and the 15th Amendment, which gave all male Americans the right to vote, regardless of their "race, color, or previous condition of

143

BLACKS TERRORIZED BY THE KU KLUX KLAN: The Klansmen, aiming in Reconstruction Days to establish white supremacy in the South, beat up blacks to discourage them from voting whenever elections were held.

servitude." But half of the adult population and half of the matriarchal slave society, those human beings who happened to be women, were ignored and told that they were hardly citizens.

CARPETBAGGERS AND SCALAWAGS

The Republicans had only to wait until 1868, when General Ulysses S. Grant of Ohio was elected President, to get what they wanted. In no time, the Southern states came under the rule of freed blacks, who were often illiterate; of "carpetbaggers" (Northern adventurers with an eye for ideals and loot); and of "scalawags" (Southern white rascals who joined the Republican party). H. C. Warmouth, a carpetbagger, who had chalked up a bad record as a Union officer in the war, became governor of Louisiana and stole $500,000 from the state's school fund, before he was caught and sent to jail. Although the Reconstruction governments in the South did manage to build public schools and promote the construction of railroads, heavy taxation ruined the plantation economy and brought about sharecropping and tenant farming, by which a farmer could scarcely earn a living. The carpetbaggers and scalawags, who made themselves rich, paid no taxes at all.

WHITE SUPREMACY

The stubborn white resistance in the South, and the use of such organizations as the Ku Klux Klan to terrorize blacks and discourage them from voting, broke the Republicans' will to enforce the 14th and 15th Amendments, and impose one-party rule on those who lived south of Washington, D.C. Gradually, conservative and racist Democrats gained control of the governments of the Southern states until, by 1877, a compromise was reached. Federal troops, stationed in various parts of the South to maintain law and order, were withdrawn; and white supremacy was recognized in the solid Democratic South, which, in turn, cooperated with Northern Republican capitalists rather than with Western farmers.

CONSERVATIVE ALLIANCE

At this time, an alliance began between conservative Northern Republicans and conservative Southern Democrats that was to put a block in the Senate on almost every progressive President, until Lyndon B. Johnson of Texas moved into the White House in 1963. So long as the Northerners kept the federal government from giving blacks the full rights of citizenship in the South, the Southerners would keep the federal government from regulating monopolies in the North.

23

GRANT'S "GILDED AGE"

"It looks as if the Republican party were going to the dogs. . . . I believe that it is today the most corrupt . . . political party that ever existed."

Senator James W. Grimes of Iowa was guilty of no exaggeration when he made that statement in a letter to Senator Lyman Trumbull of Illinois, one year after General Ulysses S. Grant of Ohio became President in 1869. The scandals and corruptions that took place in Grant's Administration were equaled only by those of President Warren G. Harding's 52 years later, and outdone only by those of Watergate 103 years later. The general, an honest, dull man, could lead soldiers by the force of his will in war, but allowed himself to be misled by corrupt politicians and profiteers in peace.

GRAFTERS IN GOVERNMENT

Two notorious moneymen, Jay Gould and Jim Fisk, attempted to corner the gold market in the New York Stock Exchange; and, with the connivance of persons high in the confidence of the President, almost got away with it. On "Black Friday," September 24, 1869, the two Wall Streeters managed, via some clever manipulation, to boost the price of gold to a record high, reaping a fortune for themselves and causing a loss of millions of dollars to scores of stockbrokers and investors. Swinging into action, the government dumped $4 million in gold on the market, and the corner collapsed; but Grant was blamed for having allowed himself to become enmeshed in the nasty business. "The worst scandals of the 18th century," wrote historian Henry Adams, "were relatively harmless by the side of this which smirched the executive, judiciary, banks, corporate systems, professions, and people, all the great active forces of society."

The Treasury Department, under Grant, farmed out uncollected taxes to private tax gatherers, who made a good thing of it, until Secretary of the Treasury William A. Richardson was investigated by Congress and forced to quit in 1874.

A St. Louis "Whisky Ring," organized by a group of distillers in 1875, was found to have cheated the federal government out of more than $3 million in taxes, with the collusion of General John McDonald, a Treasury Department official, and General Orville E. Babcock, the President's private secretary. Despite Grant's intention to "let no guilty man escape," most of them did, Babcock and McDonald included.

Thomas Murphy, a "drinking buddy" and racetrack associate of the President, who had been given the job of tax collector for the custom house in New York City, made the most of a system in which he used the influence of the White House to obtain a monopoly in the storage of imported goods. When it came out that Murphy was making huge profits for himself by charging a month's rent for one day's storage in the Port of New York, Grant reluctantly sacked him, but praised his "honesty."

Navy yards were literally riddled with graft. Commander Alfred T. Mahan testified during a Congressional investigation that a million feet of lumber purchased by the Boston Navy Yard had simply "disappeared," and that the famous yacht *America* had been remodeled for Congressman Benjamin F. Butler of Massachusetts at the taxpayers' expense.

General William W. Belknap, who served as Grant's Secretary of War, received a "kickback" of almost $25,000 from the man whom he appointed to run the Indian trading post at Fort Sill, Oklahoma, and, when caught spending the money, resigned to avoid impeachment in 1876.

The Department of the Interior was a happy hunting ground for land speculators.

The Supreme Court, influenced by big business, defended large corporations against any regulation, by declaring that they had the constitutional rights of an individual.

"Boss" William Tweed, the head of Tammany Hall and leader of the Democratic party in New York City, shamelessly "robbed" the metropolis of some $30 million, using the money to keep himself in power, protect lawbreakers, "buy" voters, and bribe members of the state Legislature.

Gambling, drinking, and whoring were popular pastimes for men of every social class.

Well did writer Mark Twain call this the "Gilded Age," for when the gilt wore off, one found only plain brass; everyone was trying to make a "fast buck."

CORRUPT CONGRESSMEN

Of all the public scandals that rocked Grant's Administration, none attracted more attention than that of the Credit Mobilier of America, a camouflaged construction company organized by the promoters of the Union Pacific Railroad so that they could divert the

LIFE WAS LIVELY, with men of every social class spending plenty of money for the popular pastimes of the day.

profits of railway construction to themselves. Fearful that a threatened 1872 Congressional investigation might blow the lid off the whole operation, Thomas C. Durant of New York City, the chief promoter, got Congressman Oakes Ames of Massachusetts to sell shares of Credit Mobilier stock to members of Congress at par, although they were worth at least twice as much in the market. The two schemers, aiming to place the shares "where they would do the most good," even lent the lawmakers money with which to buy the stock. The earnings were fabulous, and those who were in on the deal received about $3,500 for each $1,000 that they invested. Nobody, including Durant and Ames, ever wound up in jail.

THE COLFAX CASE

Schuyler Colfax of Indiana, who had served as a Congressman before becoming Grant's Vice President, was accused by Congressional investigators of having taken a bribe during his tenure as Speaker of the House of Representatives, by accepting 20 shares of stock in the infamous Credit Mobilier. "The Christian statesman," as he was called, unconvincingly denied that he had ever done such a thing. The investigators then also discovered that the Indianian had accepted an 1868 campaign contribution of $4,000 from a contractor who had supplied envelopes to the federal government at a time when he was chairman of the Committee on Post Offices and Post Roads.

The House Judiciary Committee, investigating whether the House should impeach Colfax, concluded that impeachment was "intended by the Constitution not as a way to punish malefactors, but only to remove a man from an office he has abused while occupying it." Since whatever crime Colfax had committed occurred while he was the Speaker of the House—and before he became Vice President—he could not be impeached. Not too surprisingly, Grant dumped him and picked Senator Henry Wilson of Massachusetts as his running mate when he ran for re-election in 1872.

OFFICIALS BRIBED

Until the 17th Amendment to the Constitution required popular election from 1913 on, United States Senators were chosen by state Legislatures—and, naturally, they chose men whom their rich and influential constituents paid them best to choose.

In consequence, few men reached the Senate without financial backing by one or more of the big-money "interests," such as iron and steel, railroading, oil, mining, textiles, meat packing, and sugar refining. The

industrial leaders got what they wanted for the
and the bribery of government officials and judges
merely a small part of the evil practices that they in
dulged in.

Senator Roscoe Conkling of New York, Congressman
James A. Garfield of Ohio, Senator James G. Blaine of
Maine, and other political leaders during Grant's
Administration owned stock in many large corporations
and promoted the passing of laws that worked much to
their benefit. All of them became very wealthy. A few,
such as William Tweed, wound up in jail.

DEPRESSION HITS

Heavy speculation in stocks and bonds, the over-
rapid growth of the West, and a world-wide drop in
prices brought on a severe depression in 1873, which
lasted three years. In 1876, just before economic
recovery took place, America celebrated her 100th
birthday by staging a World's Fair in Philadelphia.
Sidney Lanier, a musician and writer, contributed the
words for a Centennial musical, which ended on a high
note of optimism. But James Russell Lowell, a New
England poet, who 11 years earlier had written "O
Beautiful! My Country! Ours once more!", penned a
sarcastic lyric poem, which was much more appropriate
for the occasion:

Show your State Legislatures; show your Rings;
And challenge Europe to produce such things
As high officials sitting half in sight
To share the plunder and to fix things right;
If that don't fetch her, why you only need
To show your latest style in martyrs—Tweed!

24
CORRUPTION
EXTENDED

The Presidential election of 1876, described by historians as one of the most crooked in American history, involved, surprisingly enough, two of the most honest politicians of the day: Rutherford B. Hayes, a Republican from Ohio, and Samuel J. Tilden, a Democrat from New York. Neither of the candidates would have ever approved of the hanky-panky that was pulled off by his party.

ELECTION DEAL

Tilden, who suffered from poor health and did not really want the Presidency, won the majority of the popular vote, and, on the face of the returns, a clear majority in the electoral vote as well. But the returns from South Carolina, Florida, Louisiana, and Oregon were in dispute, and without those four states, Tilden had only 184 electoral votes; if the Republicans carried them, Hayes would have 185.

The Republicans, out to win at any cost, made a deal with the Democrats, promising that if Hayes were to become President, they would, in turn, get him to appoint a Southerner to his Cabinet, to support internal improvements in the South, and to close his eyes to the

152

15th Amendment to the Constitution, which guaranteed civil rights to blacks. The bargain was kept by both parties. An Electoral Commission, which was set up by Congress to settle the dispute, rejected the Democratic returns from the four doubtful states, and, by a strict party vote, declared Hayes the winner. But even with the disputed states counted as Republican, Tilden still had a plurality of 250,000 votes over Hayes. No question about it, both the Republicans and the Democrats were guilty of dishonesty.

Hayes, disliked by professional politicians and ridiculed because of his wife's refusal to serve alcoholic beverages in the White House, was succeeded by James A. Garfield, another Ohio Republican, who was severely criticized by the press for having accepted campaign contributions from government employees. But Garfield, who boasted about his having climbed the ladder of success "from a log cabin to the White House," was assassinated by a disappointed office seeker, within a few months after his inauguration. His Vice President and fellow Republican, Chester A. Arthur of New York, then lived in a dead man's shoes for three years, until the Democrats squeezed in with their one successful candidate between 1856 and 1912, Grover Cleveland of New York, who managed to survive the scandal of fathering an illegitimate child. He spent two terms in office, split by the Administration of Benjamin Harrison, another Ohio Republican, and was then followed by yet another Ohio Republican, William McKinley, whom historian Samuel Eliot Morison described as "a kindly soul in a spineless body."

CORRUPT CITY BOSSES

The corruption of urban politics at this time had never been equalled in American history. Imitating the example that had been set by "Boss" Tweed of New

York, city bosses in Boston, Philadelphia, and other places gained control of the immigrant vote and delivered it in a block to the candidate of their choice, in return for jobs for "loyal voters" and contracts for public works for themselves. Excusing the city bosses for their corruption, James Bryce, a well-known British commentator on life in the United States, wrote: "They are the offspring of a system. Their morality is that of their surroundings. They see a door open to wealth and power, and they walk in. The festering . . . immigrant slums of the American cities gave the bosses their opportunity, and, like good Americans, they took it. To them, politics was merely a means for getting . . . places."

THE FORGOTTEN WEST

The War Between the States had been so horrible that no one wanted a repetition of the conflict. Most Americans, and certainly most politicians, knew full well that they could make more money in peace than

IMMIGRANTS WERE PROMISED OPPORTUNITY in the "land of the free," but many of them wound up living in ghettos and slums.

they could in war. They also knew that, in order to keep the peace, the Republicans in the North would have to sacrifice their power in the South, and that the Democrats in the South would have to give way to the big business interests of the North. The West, left out in the cold by the Northern and Southern coalition in Congress, went along with newly formed political parties, such as the Greenbackers, Populists, and Prohibitionists, which sometimes won minor elections and worried the Republicans and Democrats. The anger, which arose in small towns as a result of agricultural depressions, largely helped the new parties to gain local victories; no less than two "new ideas"—the closing of saloons and votes for women—originated in the West.

BIG BUSINESS RUNS RAMPANT

Big business, helped by swindling Congressmen and obliging Republicans in the White House, exploited the nation and its natural resources until the end of the 19th century—and longer. The activities of the profiteers and the speed of industrial development were almost unbelievable. The life of the average American, greatly influenced by all of this, changed considerably. Almost everything that he ate and wore, the furnishings of his home, the tools he used, the things he turned to for recreation, and the transportation he employed were either made or controlled by giant trusts, or monopolies, whose operators acted like dictators in the production and pricing of goods. When he left his bed to have breakfast, he filled his morning lamp with kerosene produced by John D. Rockefeller's Standard Oil Trust, ate bacon packed by Philip D. Armour's Armour & Company, sweetened his coffee with sugar refined by Henry O. Havemeyer's American Sugar Refining Company, sprinkled his eggs with salt supplied by the Michigan Salt Trust, smoked a cigarette packaged by

James B. Duke's American Tobacco Company, and rode to work over rails made by Andrew Carnegie's Carnegie Steel Company. In time, many small businesses and industries were driven to the wall, or simply swallowed up.

John D. Rockefeller, whose Standard Oil Company outranked all other trusts as the most successful, secured his monopoly by methods that were frowned upon by the most tolerant businessmen of his day, and pronounced criminal by the courts. By playing competing railroads against each other, he obtained rebates from their published freight rates, and even forced them to pay Standard Oil excesses that they obtained from his competitors' freight bills. Put out of business by the Ohio courts, the company promptly re-incorporated as a holding company under the more generous laws of New Jersey and went on its merry way. Before the end of the 19th century, Rockefeller had eliminated most of his competitors, accumulated a tremendous fortune, and established the greatest monopoly in the nation.

The United States Steel Corporation, organized by steelman Charles M. Schwab and banker J. P. Morgan in 1901, "absorbed" dozens of iron and steel establishments, including Andrew Carnegie's, and gained control of about 60 per cent of the steel business in the United States. The crafty Carnegie, eager to retire, walked out of the deal with almost $500 million for himself.

UNREGULATED RAILROADS

Of all the giant corporations, the greatest in power, and the most notorious for their abuse of it, were the great railway corporations. A railroad could make or break an industry or community merely by juggling freight rates. The funds at the disposal of the railroaders, often created by the sale of stock that was not really worth the asking price, often dwarfed the budgets of state governments. Unable to recognize any public interest distinct from their own, Cornelius Vanderbilt (New York Central), Edward H. Harriman (Union Pacific), James J. Hill (Great Northern), Leland Stanford (Central Pacific), and Collis P. Huntington (Southern Pacific) had no qualms about bribing and corrupting Congressmen to get their own way in the running of their railroads, charge whatever they pleased for the carrying of freight and passengers, and evade taxation as well as regulation. No man dared engage in any business in which transportation largely entered without first obtaining the permission of a railroad manager. No politician ever got very far in politics without the "blessing" of a railroad overlord.

LAWS GO UNENFORCED

While big business dragged the Presidents by their coattails in its wake, the federal government did little at home or abroad to justify newspaper headlines. The Interstate Commerce Act and the Sherman Antitrust Act, passed by Congress in 1887 and 1890 to regulate the operation of railroads and to break up the trusts and monopolies, turned out to be nothing but delusions and shams, because they were not enforced. Federal troops were used to put down strikes; federal credit and currency remained tight and tied to the gold standard; the government was vindictive toward the poor and gave them no relief; and states' rights were set aside by the Supreme Court, in the interests of Washington lawmakers and large corporations. Leading a march of unemployed on the nation's capital to petition the enactment of "remedial legislation" in 1894, Ohioan Jacob S. Coxey was arrested for "trespassing" while delivering a speech from the steps of the Capitol.

LABOR FIGHTS BACK

Workers, organizing themselves under the banner of the Knights of Labor and striking for better working conditions and higher wages, often lost their lives while doing battle with the private armies that were hired by industrial giants to fight organized labor. Immigrant and child wage earners, exploited by ruthless employers, worked like slaves six days a week and received little pay. Yet, the vast mass of American workers preferred to fight their bosses individually rather than to work as "regimented unionists." Poorly managed by its leaders, the Knights of Labor gradually faded out. It was not until 1881, when the American Federation of Labor was founded, that the labor movement got anywhere.

Two railroads, the Baltimore & Ohio and the Pennsylvania, twice reduced wages by 10 per cent, and thereby provoked a labor conflict in 1877 that quickly spread to other railways. Unorganized railroad employees, supported by a huge army of hungry and desperate unemployed, played havoc with transportation, and during one week, every industrial center in the nation was in a turmoil. In Pittsburgh and Chicago, rioters fought pitched battles with militiamen, and some $5 million worth of property was destroyed. Federal troops had to be called in to restore order. Few people realized that America had reached a stage of industrial development that gave rise to a labor problem, or that the "Great Strike of '77" would be the first of a long series of battles between employers and employees.

In 1886, employees at the Chicago plant of the McCormick Harvester Machine Company, striking for an eight-hour working day, staged a demonstration in the city's Haymarket Square, during which someone threw a bomb, killing eight policemen and wounding 67 others. The immediate aftermath of the affair was the arrest of 10 men, who were accused of being

EMPLOYERS EXPLOITED CHILD WAGE EARNERS and immigrants who worked like slaves and received little pay.

anarchists, bent on overthrowing the government. Two were released. But of the eight who were found guilty, one committed suicide, four were hanged, and three went to prison. Convinced of their innocence, Governor John P. Altgeld pardoned the three survivors. Widely denounced as an abettor of anarchy, he was forced to give up his political career.

BLOODY HOMESTEAD

The strike against the Carnegie Steel Company at Homestead, Pennsylvania, in 1892 was particularly bloody, as was the one against the Pullman Company at Chicago in 1894. Both of them involved violent disputes over unionism, working conditions, and wages, and claimed the lives of dozens of strikers and strikebreakers alike. The Carnegie strike, during which the company used armed industrial guards supplied by the Pinkerton Detective Agency, had all of the earmarks of an all-out war, and was not broken until the governor called out the National Guard. Equally violent was the Pullman strike, which paralyzed the railroads throughout much of the North and West. Seeing it as "a war against the nation and society," President Cleveland ordered federal troops to run the trains, saying to those

159

BLOOD SPILLED AT HOMESTEAD, Pennsylvania, when Andrew Carnegie used armed industrial guards against the striking workers of his steel mill.

who pleaded on behalf of the unionized workers: "You might as well ask me to dissolve the government of the United States."

WHITE UNIONS

The American Federation of Labor, now headed by Samuel Gompers, recruited some 500,000 members and fought hard for recognition, higher wages, the closed shop, and a shorter work week. But neither Gompers nor any other trade union leader did anything to help black wage earners; all were as much against associating with colored men as any Southerner was.

The promise of opportunity in the "land of the free" attracted thousands upon thousands of immigrants from northern, southern, and eastern Europe. The railroads, now carrying passengers and freight from one side of the nation to the other, would not have been built without the Irish and Chinese, nor the steel industry without the Poles and Bohemians. Cities swelled with growing ghettos and slums. Even the wild West beckoned foreign settlers.

160

America, taking her first step to acquire more real estate outside of her natural frontiers, had bought Alaska from Russia in 1867, thus outflanking the British in Canada; and with the colonizing of the Midway Islands in the same year and the annexing of Hawaii in 1898, she had more than 50 island outposts in the Pacific. The nation that had once held the lamp of liberty, and opened its doors to refugees from oppression, was now about to become the defender of imperialism and the advocate of reactionary governments in foreign lands, all in the guise of protecting its own liberty.

25
THE "GAY" NINETIES

In 1890, with almost a whole generation having grown up since the War Between the States, America was still largely composed of scattered rural towns and cities that hardly knew or understood each other. Although most of the tens of thousands of new immigrants from Europe had remained in coastal cities, nearly three fifths of the 63 million Americans still lived in villages or on farms. Equality of opportunity was an illusion destroyed by the moneymen and profiteers. One per cent of the population owned more than 50 per cent of the national wealth, while wage earners worked away their lives in factories and sweatshops for a few cents an hour. Blacks and Indians were still being denied rights enjoyed by whites; Jews were still being denied rights enjoyed by Christians. And to top off the 1890's, America went to war with Spain.

THE UNTAXABLE RICH

The moneymen, who were able to make 10 per cent on their investments without having to pay any income tax, really lived it up in the Gay Nineties. New York City, the favorite hangout of the wealthy, became the social court of the nation. "Not to have received an

162

invitation to a millionaire's ball or dinner party," as the minister of one of the city's fashionable churches put it, "was in the 'polite world' equal to a sentence of banishment for life." The "terms of admission" were not exacting, for how could they be in a land of newly made rich?

Jay Gould, widely feared because of his financial power and influence with Congressmen, might be refused a membership in a high-class private club, but his sons, George and Edwin, would be quickly admitted. The bad-mannered railroader Cornelius Vanderbilt was unthinkable in a fancy living room, but his grandsons had all doors open to them. Steelman Andrew Carnegie, playing golf with book publisher Frank N. Doubleday, asked him: "How much did you make last month, Frank?" The publisher said that it was impossible for him to tell. "I'd get out of that business," the steelman said.

It was no longer considered "bad taste" to talk about one's bank account or one's neighbor's, or about the amount that banker J. P. Morgan paid out to run his million-dollar yacht, the *Corsair*.

The wealthy, as described by historian Henry Adams, were scarcely fit to bring up their own children. "They, who expended all their energy in the exploiting of a railroad system, of machinery, of a power plant for the new continent, had had no time for thought. . . . Their lives were generally no more worth living than those of their cooks."

THE VANISHING AMERICANS

The Dawes Act of 1887, which established the policy of breaking up Indian reservations into 160-acre individual farms, failed to "Americanize" the red men, and fold them into the body politic of the nation as it was supposed to do. Passed as the result of a great deal

SOME INDIANS BECAME RICH when oil was discovered on their land, but for most of them, life was very difficult.

of prodding by Indian rights societies that wished the Indians well, the law was largely based on the "Protestant ethic" that the ownership of real estate was for a moral good, fostering thrift and industry, and that it would provide a spark of ambition, leading to power and riches.

But the "do-gooders" completely overlooked the fact that the Indians, by habit and heredity, were hunters, not farmers, and that their ideas of land ownership were communal, not individual. Most of the Indians, preferring their way of life to that of the white man, chose to live on reservations rather than to settle down on farms. To be sure, some Indians, such as those who lived on the Osage reservation in Oklahoma, discovered oil on their lands and became very wealthy; but for most of them, life was very difficult. Many babies died shortly after they were born; many adults, suffering from diseases that they had caught from whites, never lived to reach old age. It was not until 1924 that the United States gave these vanishing "first Americans" their citizenship, and 1948 before all of the states agreed that they were, indeed, Americans.

LEGALIZED SEGREGATION

The dark people of America knew no darker years than those which brought the 19th century to an end.

Jim Crowism, or anti-black sentiment, prevented colored people from mixing with whites on trains and in public places. White nurses were forbidden to take care of black patients in hospitals, or vice versa; all colored people were barred, except as cooks and waiters, from lunch counters, bars, and restaurants run by whites; blacks could not make contracts, serve on juries, own guns, or assemble without whites standing by; colored barbers were forbidden to cut the hair of white women and children; and when taxicabs were introduced, a colored driver, if he managed to get a license, was not allowed to carry white passengers.

The Supreme Court of the United States, upholding the principle of segregation, ruled that it was perfectly legal to separate blacks from whites, provided each race enjoyed "equal facilities."

JEWS REJECTED BY CHRISTIANS

Many Jews, coming from Europe with the hope of finding a better way of life in democratic 19th-century America, were sadly disappointed when they discovered that there were many Christian employers, landlords, and businessmen who rejected them. Christian private schools refused admission to their sons and daughters. Christian clubs blackballed their membership applications. In short, they found the same anti-Semitism in American towns and cities as they had found in European towns and cities.

Henry Hilton, the manager of the Grand Union, a famous summer hotel at Saratoga, New York, refused Jewish guests, contending that the establishment's Christian patrons "did not want Israelites around the place."

There was a threat of action under the New York civil rights law, but Hilton successfully defended the hotel's position by declaring: "The law yet permits a man to use his property as he pleases, and I propose to exercise that blessed privilege, notwithstanding that Moses and all his descendants might object. . . . Personally, I have no particular feeling on the subject, except probably that I don't like this class as a general thing and don't care whether they like me or not. . . . I believe we lose much more than we gain by their custom."

The Hilton-Israelite controversy had scarcely quieted down when Austin Corbin, the president of both the Long Island Railroad and a real estate company that was working with the railway to develop Coney Island into a fashionable resort, made this blunt announcement: "We do not like Jews as a class. There are some well-behaved people among them, but as a rule they make themselves offensive to the kind of people who principally patronize our railroad and hotel, and I am satisfied we should be better off without than with their custom."

One happy result, emerging from all of this, was that the Reverend Henry Ward Beecher, a Protestant clergyman and the brother of Harriet Beecher Stowe, the author of *Uncle Tom's Cabin*, became an outspoken champion of the Jews and greatly influenced millions of Christians to change their attitude toward them. In one statement, he referred to the anti-Semitic patrons of the Grand Union Hotel as "men who made their money yesterday, or a few years ago, selling codfish"; in another, he advised the Jews to ignore the insults: "A hero may be annoyed by a mosquito, but to put on his whole armor and call on his followers to join him in making war on an insect would be beneath his dignity."

AMERICA TURNS IMPERIALIST

President William McKinley did not want to go to war with Spain, particularly since there was no real proof that the Spaniards had blown up one of America's favorite battleships, the *U.S.S. Maine*, in Havana harbor. But Congress and the press, and "young Republicans" like Senator Henry Cabot Lodge of Massachusetts and Assistant Secretary of the Navy Theodore Roosevelt, were clamoring for a fight, and McKinley, fearing that the Republican party might be broken up if he did not give way to it, decided to yield. One year later he confessed that "a peaceful solution might have been had."

The Spanish-American War of 1898, which turned Spain's empire into shambles, ended with America's acquiring Cuba, which she held until 1902, when the island became an independent nation; the Philippines, for which she paid the Spaniards $20 million; and the islands of Guam and Puerto Rico, which she got for nothing.

Two years later, in 1900, American troops were sent to China to help put down the Boxer Rebellion, beginning a more direct policy of American intervention in the affairs of Asia. The United States, now the world's largest producer of food, coal, iron, and steel, was not to escape the contagion of imperialism that had begun to block out the globe into spheres of European influence and captive markets. As Senator Albert J. Beveridge of Indiana summed it: "Fate has written our policy for us . . . the trade of the world must and shall be ours."

The Republican party held all of the trump cards —military victory, world prestige, and booming prosperity—in the Presidential election of 1900. McKinley, of course, was put up for a second term, and, in a move to isolate the troublesome Teddy Roosevelt, the bosses saw to it that he was nominated for the Vice Presidency. But, much to the sorrow of the "Grand Old Party," McKinley was shot to death by an anarchist within a few months after his second inauguration, and Theodore Roosevelt became President.

26

TEDDY THE TRUST BUSTER

Theodore Roosevelt, who held the Presidency for seven years after William McKinley's assassination in 1901, came as close to being a king as the Constitution of the United States allowed him to be. So lively and "bully" (his favorite word) was the young President, who had just turned 43, that many of his fellow Republicans saw him as radical and reckless. But impulsive as he was, Teddy was always willing to compromise with Congress, particularly if there was a chance of his having his own way in the end.

He had scarcely been sworn into office when he called for enforcement of existing laws regarding trusts and monopolies, and asked for full power of the federal government to inspect and regulate corporations engaged in interstate commerce. But as much as he talked against the giant industrialists and profiteers, he achieved little, except for creating a few headline-making cases, such as the Northern Securities Company.

Although Teddy liked to appear as a man of action, his principles, as writer Mark Twain observed, looked so much like "expedient policies" that they had the same "quality of impermanency, a disposition to fade and

169

disappear at convenience." T.R. did, indeed, push through some progressive legislation during his Administration, but only when a scandal or a crying need for reform prodded him hard enough. If his foreign policy was to "speak softly and carry a big stick," his domestic policy was to speak loudly and carry a toothpick.

"BULLY" FOR BIG BUSINESS

American democracy, although not endangered by a foreign enemy, was gravely menaced by the greed of the trusts and monopolies when Theodore Roosevelt took over the Presidency. Republican bosses like Senators Thomas C. Platt of New York and Mark Hanna of Ohio insisted that the government keep its hands off big business. The chief function of the President and Congress, as they saw it, was to help business, not to inquire into its practices—and above all, not to inquire into its method of making profits. Opposing the thinking of the "Old Guard" Republicans were the Progressives, led by Senator Robert M. LaFollette of Wisconsin, who viewed the trusts and monopolies with heated hostility, declaring them to be the "gravest danger menacing our free institutions." Between those who wanted big business to be left alone and those who wished it to be controlled, Roosevelt made himself the spokesman of the middle course. His fat, weak successor, William Howard Taft, prosecuted twice as many monopolists in four years as he did in seven.

T.R. AND LABOR

Roosevelt's attitude toward organized labor was ambiguous. He supported the unions in their demands for higher wages and shorter hours, but he believed in the "open shop" and resented what he called the unionists' "arrogant and domineering attitude."

In 1902 there came a test case—the strike in the Pennsylvania coal mines of the Philadelphia & Reading Coal & Iron Company, which was largely controlled by banker J. P. Morgan, the Vanderbilts, and A. J. Cassatt, the president of the Pennsylvania Railroad. Roosevelt, pressured by reformers who objected to the dirty deal that the miners were getting, called a meeting which included G. F. Baer, the president of the mining company, and John Mitchell, the president of the United Mine Workers. The union offered to arbitrate, but the company refused.

The President, now aroused to the utmost, compelled the company to submit to arbitration by a government committee. The committee, investigating the mining operation, found appalling working conditions and acceded to the demands of the strikers for a nine-hour day and a 10 per cent wage increase, meanwhile denying recognition of their union. Baer, furious, summed up his feelings in a declaration that epitomized forever the concept of the "divine right" held over labor by mine operators: "The rights and interests of the laboring man will be protected and cared for by the Christian men to whom God has given control of the property rights of the country. Pray earnestly that right may triumph, always remembering that the Lord God Omnipotent still reigns."

RIGHTING WRONGS

While waiting for legislation to strengthen the Interstate Commerce Commission so that it could better regulate the railroads, Roosevelt found plenty of work to do in eliminating the corruption in government that had been taking place since the War Between the States. Dishonest employees in the Post Office Department were uncovered and punished. Upton Sinclair's best-selling 1906 book, *The Jungle*, drew popular as well as

171

FILTHY FOOD WAS ALLOWED to be sold, until the Pure Food and Drug Act of 1906 forced meat packers and other food producers to clean up their plants.

Presidential attention to disgusting conditions in the meat-packing houses of Chicago and gave vent to a government investigation, while Dr. H. W. Wiley, a chemist in the Department of Agriculture, proved by tests the dangerous effects of preservatives and coloring matter in canned foods. The big food companies fought hammer and tongs against such "Socialist interference." ("It don't hurt the kids," said a candy manufacturer who diluted his coconut bars with shredded bone, "they like it.") But Congress did its duty, for a change, and passed the Pure Food and Drug Act of 1906, which, despite the fact that it was never fully enforced, gave consumers some measure of protection.

"FIXES"

The Northern Securities Company, organized by J. P. Morgan, E. H. Harriman, and James J. Hill to gain control of competing railroads in the Northwest, so blatantly violated the Sherman Antitrust Act of 1890 that Roosevelt was forced to order his Attorney General, Philander C. Knox, to take action against the group.

Morgan, angered by the government's move against one of his favorite interests, paid a visit to the White House and brazenly stood up against the President: "If we have done anything wrong, send your man (meaning Knox) to see my man (meaning his lawyer), and they can fix it up." Roosevelt objected; and Knox, a former lawyer for the notorious Carnegie Steel Company, who now found himself playing a strange, new role, asserted that the purpose of the proceeding was not to "fix" things.

Leading newspapers posed the question: Would the Supreme Court of the United States, which had so often taken sides with trusts and monopolies, sustain the "trust-busting" President? The nation waited for the Court's awful judgment, while Roosevelt himself suffered a great deal of anxiety. Finally, after two years of costly litigation, on March 14, 1904, the order to dissolve the company came from the Justices, by a close 5-to-4 vote.

The arguments were soon forgotten. In the Presidential election that took place later in the year, Morgan, Harriman, and Hill were among the largest contributors to Roosevelt's campaign chest.

USING A "BIG STICK"

The world worried, for a time, about Roosevelt's using a "big stick" to further American political and economic "imperialism," even to conquer fresh territory in the Americas. Much to the relief of many people, he evacuated Cuba and initiated self-government in the Philippines, both of which had been taken over by the United States at the end of the Spanish-American War in 1898. But the method that he used to bring about America's building of the Panama Canal has yet to be forgotten by the Latin Americans.

The Isthmus of Panama, through which the canal was to pass, was part of Colombia, and that republic was reluctant to part with any of her real estate. President Roosevelt, using trickery, encouraged the Panamanians to rebel against the Colombians and to set up a new Republic of Panama. Colombia, threatened by three American warships that suddenly appeared on the scene, quickly gave up any idea of fighting things out. The United States immediately recognized Panama as an independent nation, and agreed to pay her $10 million down and an annual rental of $250,000 in return for a lease on a six-mile-wide strip of land that came to be known as the "Canal Zone."

By marrying the Atlantic with the Pacific, the canal, which was built after great difficulty, opened in 1914, shortening a ship's route between America's East and West Coasts by thousands of miles. Seven years later, in 1921, the United States finally paid Colombia $25 million for the loss of her property. But great harm had been done to America's reputation. Could she now deny that she was imperialistic?

DOLLAR DIPLOMACY

Roosevelt also saw fit to wield a big stick elsewhere in the Caribbean, claiming the right to send armed forces into any Latin-American country that made so bold as to have a revolution or to threaten American property interests. President Taft, following the same course, continued this policy of "dollar diplomacy," as did President Woodrow Wilson, who had no qualms about intervening in the internal affairs of Mexico, Nicaragua, Haiti, and the Dominican Republic. Whatever chance there had been for a good relationship with Latin America went completely down the drain.

T.R. STRENGTHENS JAPAN

President Roosevelt's decision to act as mediator in the Russo-Japanese War (1904–5) probably saved Japan from a beating, but her government and press persuaded her people that the Rooseveltian big stick had done her out of huge territorial gains. The Treaty of Portsmouth, largely engineered by the President at the end of the conflict, established Japan as top dog in Manchuria and enabled her to become the dominant naval power in the Pacific. A few years later, in 1910, she violated the treaty and annexed Korea. During World War II, the United States paid heavily for the long-term results of Theodore Roosevelt's meddling, for which, ironically enough, he was awarded the Nobel peace prize.

Not too surprisingly, the Republicans drew a sigh of relief in 1909, when Roosevelt handed over the keys of the White House to William Howard Taft, and announced that he was going to Africa to hunt big game.

27

PROFESSOR AT THE HELM

Fed up with Republican William Howard Taft's "indifferent performance" in the White House, and afraid that Theodore Roosevelt, now the Presidential hopeful of the new Progressive party, was still a Republican at heart, the voters gave Woodrow Wilson, a Democratic reformer and ex-president of Princeton University, an overwhelming victory in the election of 1912. But, contrary to what many historians have said in praising him for the political, economic, and social reforms that he managed to put through during his two terms in office, President Wilson was at no time motivated by a real love for people in general. Always aloof, he preferred privacy to company and had only a few close friends. Teddy Roosevelt once described him as "a very adroit and able (but not forceful) hypocrite."

A DISAPPOINTED PUBLIC

Secretary of State William Jennings Bryan and other progressive-thinking Democrats were sadly disappointed when Wilson failed to come up with legislation to destroy the financial cliques of New York and Boston, regulate the stock exchanges, place a heavy tax on large

176

corporations, and establish more stringent controls over giant trusts and monopolies.

Blacks, who had supported Wilson in the election, got less than nothing. Racial segregation was extended to almost every federal department, and a wholesale firing of black postmasters and other minor government officials took place in the South.

Nothing was done to fight Jim Crowism, or to help Catholics in Oregon in their battle for parochial schools.

Organized labor, concerned about the growing number of incoming Europeans who were willing to work for low wages, did not get from Wilson the restriction on unlimited immigration that it had hoped to get.

The Ku Klux Klan, left free by the federal government to operate as it pleased, openly promoted nativism and "white Protestant supremacy," and practically controlled the politics of Georgia, Indiana, Maine, Oklahoma, Oregon, and Texas. Wearing white hoods and robes, and parading and burning crosses in the dark of night, the Klan equally terrorized and persecuted Catholics, Jews, immigrants, and blacks.

A RESPECTABLE PRESIDENCY

Fortunate enough to have a Democratic majority in Congress, the President was able to transfer the election of United States Senators from state Legislatures to the people, to give women the right to vote, to lower the tariff on imported goods, to regulate private banks by a newly created Federal Reserve System, to put through a personal income tax on incomes above $3,000 a year, to push through an anti-trust law, and to give legal protection to the rights of two million unionists in the American Federation of Labor. Even the reactionary Supreme Court, which had long blocked laws for economic reform, began to hand down more liberal decisions. But when Congress passed a law in 1916 to

177

prevent employers from exploiting child labor, the Court surprised everybody by saying that it was unconstitutional.

THE HANGING OF A JEW

Woodrow Wilson had scarcely finished his first year in office when his attention was drawn to Atlanta, Georgia, where Leo M. Frank, the manager of a pencil factory and leader of the city's Jewish community, was accused of attacking and killing a Christian girl. Thomas Watson, the publisher of *The Jeffersonian* and a staunch anti-Semite, led demands that Frank be hanged. Said Watson: "Lynch law is a good sign; it shows that a sense of justice yet lives among the people." Mobs, stirred up by the publisher's front-page stories condemning the accused, brought terror to Atlanta's streets. A detective, hired to help in Frank's defense, was driven out of town for "selling out to the Jews." Frank's lawyer was warned: "If they don't hang that Jew, we'll hang you." Frank was found guilty, but the governor of Georgia, believing that the trial had been unfair, changed the death sentence to life imprisonment. Frank was sent to a prison farm, where another prisoner tried to kill him with a razor.

On August 16, 1915, a half-crazed crowd took Frank from his cell and hanged him. The *Marietta Journal* told its readers: "We regard the hanging of Leo M. Frank as an act of law-abiding citizens." All too late, Frank was proved to be innocent. There was no comment from the President or from anyone else in the nation's capital.

POLICING THE LATINS

Continuing in Latin America the "dollar diplomacy" of Theodore Roosevelt and William Howard Taft, which he had once severely criticized, Woodrow Wilson came close to involving the United States in a war with
178

Mexico in 1916, when he sent 12,000 troops into that country to punish Pancho Villa, a swashbuckling bandit, who was striving for political power and threatening American property interests.

A treaty, furthering American influence in Nicaragua, so greatly curtailed that country's sovereignty that it was formally denounced by the Central American Court of Justice.

United States Marines, ordered into Haiti "to keep the peace," exacted a heavy toll of Haitian lives and remained in that country until 1930.

The Dominican Republic, under American political domination, was forced to put up with an intolerable American ambassador who acted as if he owned the place.

It was not until 1934, when President Franklin D. Roosevelt adopted a "good-neighbor" policy in the Caribbean, that the United States finally renounced her "right to intervene in the internal and external affairs" of Latin-American nations.

NEUTRALITY BACKFIRES

In 1914, when World War I broke out in Europe, President Wilson made an official proclamation of neutrality, declaring that "the United States must be neutral in fact as well as in name . . . impartial in thought as well as in action . . ." and ". . . put a curb upon our sentiments." But, as things worked out, the American people were divided emotionally before the war was a month old. A majority, still loyal to the "old country," took sides with the Allies (England, France, Italy, and Russia); but an important minority, chiefly made up of German-Americans and Irish-Americans, supported the Central European Powers (Germany and Austria-Hungary) and their allies, Turkey and Bulgaria, either out of love for the "fatherland" or out of hatred

179

for King George V of England, who was denying independence to Ireland. Scandinavian-Americans, along with Midwesterners, remained neutral, wanting no part of an Old World fight.

As the Presidential election of 1916 approached, American pressure seemed strong enough to protect American ships and war profits, as well as her citizens abroad, without committing the decisive strength of the United States to one side or the other. Because of America's threat to enter the war if neutral ships were sunk, Germany, although answering Britain's surface blockade with plenty of naval action, was not as yet engaged in unrestricted submarine warfare against all ships sailing in and out of Allied ports. Thus the Democrats, aiming to re-elect Wilson, were able to capitalize on his keeping the peace, and make use of a powerful campaign slogan—"He kept us out of war!"

But, even after being heralded as the "savior of peace," Wilson just about managed to win the election by carrying the South and West against Republican Charles Evans Hughes of New York, who made a clean sweep of the Eastern states. Less than six months after winning the election, on April 6, 1917, the President signed a declaration of war on the German Empire, telling Congress that "the world must be made safe for democracy."

Afraid that the spirit of brutality would pervade American life, Wilson had hesitated to take action, even when the Germans decided to gamble on a quick victory, and use submarines as they pleased. Only "proof" that Germany was trying to get Mexico and Japan to attack the United States, and engage her in the Caribbean and the Pacific, convinced the President to join the Allies. American intervention seemed even more necessary when the Russian front against the Germans collapsed, and news of the Russian Communist revolution and abdication of the Russian czar reached the American people. There were now four democracies, including the new Russia, fighting two autocracies and their allies; America could choose only one side.

A FAREWELL TO CIVIL LIBERTIES

On the excuse, or the belief, that America was honeycombed with secret enemy agents, Congress passed the Espionage and Sedition Acts in 1917–18, which made it a crime to print, write, or publish any "disloyal, profane, scurrilous, or abusive language about the form of government of the United States, or the Constitution . . . or the military forces . . . or the flag . . . or the uniform of the Army and Navy. . . ."

The states went even further with laws against anarchy and sedition, which, combined with federal laws against interfering with the drafting of men for the armed forces, made it a crime "to advocate heavier taxation instead of [war] bond issues . . . to state that conscription was unconstitutional . . . to say that the sinking of merchant vessels was legal . . . to urge that a referendum should have preceded our declaration of war . . ." or "to say that war was contrary to the teachings of Christ."

Under these laws, the government arrested some 1,500 Americans for disloyalty. Among those sentenced to lengthy prison terms were Eugene V. Debs of Indiana, the leader of the Socialist party, for threatening that Socialists would not support the war; and Victor L. Berger of Wisconsin, the first Socialist to be elected to Congress, for writing articles against the war. A 21-year-old girl, who passed out pamphlets attacking President Wilson and opposing America's intervention in Europe, was sentenced to 15 years in jail.

Besides the "official crusade" against sedition, there was the unofficial spy hunting that kept busybodies of

WOMEN BATTLED POLICE and lawmakers for many years, before they finally got the right to vote in 1920.

both sexes busy. Not only was it a wonderful opportunity to use "patriotism" in neighborhood quarrels, but also an ideal time to exercise personal grudges. German-Americans, who did as much to support the war effort as any other group, took the brunt of it and suffered the most. Armchair patriots, indulging in a hate campaign, even went so far as to promote the passing of state laws forbidding the teaching of German in schools and colleges, the selling of German books, and the playing of German music.

THE WAR TO END WARS

When President Wilson joined the Allies he had supposed that the security of the New World depended on the stability of the Old. He also planned that World War I would be "the war to end all wars." In a message to Congress on January 8, 1918, Wilson set out 14 points, asking for the right of self-determination in *all* European countries, freedom of the seas in peace and war, and a "general association of nations." There were to be no

182

reparations, no indemnities, and no humiliating peace terms to plant the seed for another catastrophe.

The United States won the war and lost the peace. The American voters squelched whatever chance Wilson had to carry out his plan. Annoyed at the war's having already cost America more than 50,000 men and $30 billion, they sent a Republican majority back to Congress in the elections of 1918. A few days later, on November 11, the world conflict ended, and shortly thereafter, the President sailed for France to attend the Paris Peace Conference.

Showing his stubbornness, Wilson refused to invite any Republican leaders to join him in Paris to help work out the Treaty of Versailles, although the treaty would have to be ratified by two-thirds of the Senate. He also made the big mistake of believing that, once he got back home, he would be able to get the Senators to accept the peace terms that he had negotiated, by appealing over their heads to the people. His tactics, in the words of Secretary of State Robert Lansing, were those of a "foxy ward politician." Yet, in Europe, he got most of what he wanted, including an agreement to establish the League of Nations, even when he was forced to accept an Allied indemnity against Germany (the seed of future conflict), and the confiscation of her colonies.

Returning to the United States, Wilson found many people who favored the League of Nations, which was to police the world, and thereby prevent another war. But one of his worst enemies, Republican Senator Henry Cabot Lodge of Massachusetts, with deadly cleverness, maneuvered the Senate to doom the treaty and the League. The President, realizing that his dream of making the world safe for democracy was being undermined and rendered useless, suffered a paralytic stroke on September 25, 1919, from which he never fully recovered. For at least two months, Wilson's secretary, Joseph Tumulty; the President's wife, Edith; and his personal physician, Dr. Cary T. Grayson, acted as an informal council of regency. According to the Constitution, Vice President Thomas R. Marshall should have assumed the powers and duties of the Presidency. But when this was propounded by Secretary of State Robert Lansing, Mrs. Wilson and Tumulty opposed it so vigorously that Lansing went no further. And who was to declare Presidential disability? The Constitution and the laws said nothing about that. Fortunately, from about November 1, Wilson regained full control of his mental faculties.

A CRACKDOWN ON THE "REDS" AND JEWS

Meanwhile, there were many sad happenings on the domestic front. Deciding that the way to fame and power was to crack down on the "Reds," Wilson's Attorney General, A. Mitchell Palmer, instigated a series of lawless raids on homes and labor-union offices, and, in January, 1920, arrested more than 4,000 alleged Communists in 33 different cities. The raids turned up almost nothing in the way of revolutionaries or firearms, but Palmer emerged as a national hero. In New York, where the anti-radical campaign reached its climax, the state Assembly expelled five Socialist members, although the Socialist party was legally recognized, and its members were innocent of any offense.

Henry Ford, the founder and president of the Ford Motor Company, reprinted in the *Dearborn* [Michigan] *Independent*, a newspaper he controlled, that hoary fake, *The Protocols of the Learned Elders of Zion*, which attempted to prove that there was a Jewish conspiracy to destroy civilization. Besides this, he either wrote or had written for him a book, *The International Jew* (1920), in which he blamed that race for World War I and everything else that was wrong on earth.

There were also major racial disorders in New York and Nebraska, and at least seven in the South, mostly occasioned by black war veterans who had the "impudence" to demand their rights as citizens.

The Ku Klux Klan, turning out anti-Catholic pamphlets, accused the Knights of Columbus, an international fraternal organization of Catholic men, of indulging in obscene rites.

NORMALCY

Had it not been for his illness, Woodrow Wilson might well have been nominated for a third Presidential term by the Democrats in 1920. A. Mitchell Palmer thought, for a time, that he would be nominated; but he and William G. McAdoo, the President's son-in-law, killed each other's chances, and Governor James A. Cox of Ohio won the nomination, with Franklin D. Roosevelt of New York as the Vice Presidential nominee.

The Republicans picked Senator Warren G. Harding of Ohio for President and Governor Calvin Coolidge of Massachusetts for Vice President. Harding, whom Wilson called a "bungalow mind," measured public feelings correctly when he announced, "America's present need is not heroics but healing; not nostrums but normalcy; not revolution but restoration . . . not surgery but serenity."

The voters gave Harding more than 16 million votes, and Cox less than 10 million. At least half of the some 900,000 votes polled by Socialist candidate Eugene V. Debs, who was still in jail for opposing the war, were a sign of protest by people who were disillusioned with the Democrats but unwilling to go Republican.

28
HARDING AND THE "OHIO GANG"

Whenever historians, journalists, and students discuss Warren G. Harding's Administration, the question inevitably arises as to whether it was more or less corrupt and scandal-ridden than Ulysses S. Grant's, 50 years earlier. Never is there any controversy as to whether the Nixon Administration of 50 years later turned out to be more corrupt and scandal-ridden. Next to Nixon, Harding was pale. He was a compromise candidate chosen by the Republican party leaders in a smoke-filled room, and presented to the American people as a nice guy and a fatherly figure. Harding was called by publicist George Creel and the Republican propaganda corps "a typical American and a pillar of the Baptist church." Samuel Eliot Morison, Andrew Sinclair, and other leading historians have pictured his Administration as the "worst" in American history, up to that time.

Walter Lippmann, an editor of both the *New Republic* and *New York World*, diagnosed Harding's election as "the backwash of the excitement and the sacrifice, when the people were war-weary and angry at the disappointing peace which followed World War I." Others said that disillusion over the peace, and the feeling that all of America's sacrifices had been in vain, did as much as anything else to encourage the voters to turn their backs on the Democrats.

Many people, jittery about the "Red menace," welcomed the Republican nomination of Governor Calvin Coolidge of Massachusetts for the Vice Presidency. To them, he was "the man who defied Bolshevism" by putting down the Boston police strike of 1919, the man who stood up to union-minded policemen, telling them that "there was no right to strike against the public safety by anybody, anywhere, anytime." Seeing the puritanlike New Englander as a "man of destiny," Frank Waterman Stearns, the president of a large Massachusetts dry goods firm, toured the state, declaring: "I have become convinced that the salvation of . . . the country demands that Calvin Coolidge should be kept in active public life, and as near the top as possible."

THE "HOLLOW MEN"

Harding's appointees—except for Secretary of State Charles Evans Hughes, Secretary of the Treasury Andrew W. Mellon, and Secretary of Commerce Herbert C. Hoover—were, as poet-critic T. S. Eliot observed, mostly "hollow men," who had nothing in them but "wind, greed, and a certain cunning."

Harry M. Daugherty, a member of a group of shady Republicans known as the "Ohio gang," was appointed Attorney General, but decided to make easy money by illegally selling liquor permits, and dishonestly issuing pardons to wealthy lawbreakers. All too ambitious, he was caught and quickly dismissed when Coolidge moved up from the Vice Presidency to the Presidency, upon Harding's death in 1923.

"Colonel" Charles R. Forbes, the director of the Veterans' Bureau, was forced to resign, for taking

PARTIES WERE THE THING at the White House, where the Ohio gang often carried on in a secret upstairs room from dusk to dawn.

bribes in the construction of servicemen's hospitals, and profiting from the sale of surplus war materials.

Congressman George Holden Tinkham of Massachusetts got just about anything that he wanted from the government, mainly because he had managed to buy a good 10 years' supply of whisky before the 18th Amendment to the Constitution outlawed alcoholic beverages in 1920; and with this being considered as "legal private stock," no federal agent dared to interfere with his handing it out to "influential friends," including the President himself.

Gaston B. Means, an employee of the Department of Justice, and his sidekick, Jess Smith, made themselves close to $7 million, by selling permits for "medicinal whisky," and collecting bribes from bootleggers. Means served a term in prison, and Smith committed suicide.

The Custodian of Alien Property, who had sold valuable German chemical patents for a song to his friends, was discharged from office and convicted of a criminal conspiracy to defraud the government.

Nan Britton, whose book, *The President's Daughter*, told the sordid story of how she became Harding's mistress and bore him a child, was regularly sneaked into the White House for lovemaking with the President. Mrs. Harding did her best to impose respectability on the Executive Mansion, but her husband outfoxed her by escaping to a secluded upstairs room, where, behind locked doors, he would often remain from dusk to dawn, drinking and playing poker with members of the Ohio gang. With most of the government's business being handled by his assistants, Harding did little more than serve as a "rubber stamp."

TEAPOT DOME

But scandalous as all of these happenings were, none of them received the sensational exposure that was given to the oil scandal. The evidence, obtained by a correspondent of the *St. Louis Post–Dispatch*, and made public by Senators Thomas J. Walsh of Montana and Gerald P. Nye of North Dakota, established beyond doubt the guilt of two of Harding's favorite cronies: Secretary of the Interior Albert B. Fall and Secretary of the Navy Edwin M. Denby. Fall, with the passive connivance of Denby, entered into an alliance with oilmen Edward L. Doheny and Harry F. Sinclair to turn over to them two huge government oil reserves— Teapot Dome in Wyoming and Elk Hill in California— which had been set aside for the Navy's future use. Teapot Dome was leased to Sinclair; Elk Hill, to Doheny. The leaseholders, making a show of patriotism, built a

189

few oil storage tanks for the Navy at Pearl Harbor, Hawaii; but Fall collected at least $300,000 from Sinclair and $100,000 from Doheny. The Senate, which carried out an intensive investigation, forced both Secretaries to resign and canceled the oil leases. Criminal suits were brought against Fall, Sinclair, and Doheny; but Fall was the only one convicted and sent to jail. It was also charged that some of the profits had found their way into the campaign funds of the Republican party, but little or nothing was done about that. The Government recovered $6 million from the culprits, and nothing more was done about that.

AN UNENFORCEABLE LAW

No sooner had national Prohibition, or the 18th Amendment, become law in 1920 than bootlegging sprang up to quench the public thirst. The federal government, out to keep the nation "dry" at any cost, made over half a million arrests and secured over 300,000 convictions within the short space of 10 years, but actually accomplished little in its attempt to prevent smuggling.

Speedboats, too fast for the United States Coast Guard to catch, operated out of every seaport from Maine to Florida, picking up cargoes of wine and liquor from ocean-going ships, anchored safely outside the three-mile limit.

Obliging vineyards in California and New York provided barrels of grape juice, which, with a little time and yeast cake, were easily converted into "hard stuff."

Millions of gallons of industrial alcohol, legally manufactured under the law, were turned into bootleg gin and whisky, and bottled with phony labels. Poisonous wood alcohol, poorly processed, caused blindness, insanity, or death.

Liquor and wine, imported from Europe under license

BOOZE BOATED TO BOOTLEGGERS: Speedboats, too fast for the Coast Guard to catch, flaunted the law and picked up wine and liquor from ocean-going ships for delivery to bootleggers in seacoast cities.

for "medicinal purposes," were heavily consumed by healthy men and women who were able to talk their doctors into writing prescriptions for drugstores to fill.

Saloons became "speakeasies," and almost everyone who wanted liquor had a bootlegger who kept him well supplied with alcoholic beverages.

Rhode Islanders, who refused either to ratify the 18th Amendment or to help enforce it, were able to buy their intoxicants from neighborhood groceries for $10 a bottle.

Drinkers who did not care to buy from bootleggers, and so to contribute to crime and political corruption, made their own "bathtub gin," or settled for home-brewed beer and hard cider.

Bravado encouraged many young people to drink who otherwise might never have raised a glass.

Prohibition, a dismal failure, not only increased law-breaking, but also created a criminal class that turned to gambling, drugs, and prostitution when the 18th Amendment was finally repealed in 1933.

MORALS GET LOOSER

Loose morals, which social scientists generally ascribed to World War I, really blossomed in the 1920's. Increased knowledge of sexual hygiene reduced the fear of contracting gonorrhea or syphilis. The automobile, now equipped with soft, spring cushions, was ideal for clandestine lovemaking, and country lanes became lovers' lanes. Movies, featuring scantily clad starlets such as Theda Bara, became more suggestive and sexy. Jazz, which the Reverend Henry Van Dyke of New York City's Brick Presbyterian Church called "a sensual teasing of the strings of sensual passion," was the principal dance music.

Women, tired of wearing ankle-length dresses and skirts, raised them to knee-length to look sexier. Disorderly houses, located in "red-light districts," and staffed by two-dollar whores, existed in most major cities and many towns. The Mann Act of 1910, which had been passed by Congress to keep men from transporting women from one state to another for immoral purposes, was seldom observed or enforced. More than 9,000 people were lawlessly killed each year. There were almost 50 times as many robberies in the United States as in Great Britain, and three times as many burglaries. Less than one sixth of those arrested received any punishment. Commenting on the "invasion of lawlessness," Herbert Hoover said, "Our record cannot be compared with that of other nations."

THE "WOP" CASE

In April, 1920, in the shoe-manufacturing town of South Braintree, Massachusetts, F. A. Parmenter, the paymaster of a local factory, and his guard, Alessandro Berardelli, were shot to death while attempting to prevent two armed men from robbing them of a $15,000 payroll. Police, with nothing but a telephone tip to go on, arrested Nicola Sacco and Bartolomeo Vanzetti, both of whom were immigrants from Italy, and admitted anarchists who spoke no English. Charged with murder and brought to trial before Judge Webster Thayer, in the spring of 1921, the pair were convicted, and sentenced to die in the electric chair.

The news leaked out that the judge, who was hostile to Socialists and radicals, had said privately that he would "get those Wop bastards and see them hanged." Public interest mounted, and many people began to believe that Sacco and Vanzetti were innocent, and the victims of the "Red scare." Successive stays postponed the execution, while appeals were made to the highest court in Massachusetts, and to the Supreme Court of the United States. All forms of clemency were denied. Demonstrations occurred in many American cities as well as in Europe. Bombs were set off in New York and Philadelphia, and guards were set up against other threats of violence. Maintaining their innocence, Sacco and Vanzetti were executed in August, 1927. But the haunting question of their guilt yet remains.

AMERICA FOR AMERICANS

Unlimited immigration—except for Orientals, paupers, lunatics, prostitutes and criminals—had been the accepted thing in the United States before World War I. But, with peace achieved, labor leaders began to fear that they would not be able to hold the wage gains that they had won during the war, when the average salary rose from approximately $11 to $14 per week. Intellectuals, supporting the unionists in their demand for restricted immigration, felt that an overwhelming number of immigrants from southern and eastern Europe, with different traditions and ways of life, would prove to be a menace to American society.

Kenneth Roberts, writing a series of articles for the

193

Saturday Evening Post, argued that further unrestricted immigration would flood the nation with "human parasites," and produce a "hybrid race of good-for-nothing mongrels." Many Americans—particularly those who had friends and relatives who wanted to leave Europe for the "land of opportunity"—cried out that all of this was "unjust and undemocratic"; but southern Italians were suspect, because of the Mafia's having originated in Sicily; and eastern Europeans were suspect, because of their possibly being Jewish or "Red." So Congress, aiming to please voters who wanted to keep America "100 per cent American," passed the Johnson Act of 1924, which barred Asiatics, and limited immigration from Europe to not more than 154 thousand a year. The ghettos in the Northern cities, where immigrants had largely congregated, gradually faded out; but new ones were soon created by an influx of Southern blacks and Puerto Ricans, who were already citizens of the United States. Many of these Americans, without an education or a trade, wound up on welfare, or turned to crime. According to Census Bureau figures, 10 per cent of them were illiterate.

THE ELECTION OF 1924

In the 19th century, any revelation of shenanigans, such as those that took place in Harding's Administration, would have certainly brought a violent political reaction. But Calvin Coolidge, who had acceded to the Presidency when Harding died of an embolism in 1923, miraculously restored the people's faith in the Republican party. Eager to be "President in his own right," he won the election of 1924, defeating little-known Democrat John W. Davis of West Virginia. For the next four years, America had to put up with a "do-little" Administration.

29

"SILENT CAL"

President Calvin Coolidge, often referred to as "Silent Cal," was thought by many of his Republican followers to be brighter than he was, because he seldom said anything. Although he possessed a moral integrity that was wanting in his predecessor, his political and economic policies were very little different from those of Warren G. Harding. Described by historians as "unimaginative" and as "the 'least' President America has ever had," Coolidge gave no lead to Congress, or to the nation, and took it easy in the White House, spending more time sleeping than any previous Chief Executive. By doing nothing to stop, or discourage, the wild speculation that was going on in stocks and bonds, he not only gave rise to "unregulated capitalism," but also paved the way for the disastrous stock market crash of 1929, and the Great Depression which followed it.

"THE THIN MAN"

Frank R. Kent, the managing editor of the *Baltimore Sun*, pictured Coolidge as "physically and mentally thin—thin in body, thin in spirit, thin in mind. Not bad, Good Lord, no, just thin, a thoroughly commonplace, colorless personality, with a neat, one-cylinder intellect and thoroughly precinct mind."

COOLIDGE LIKED TO SLEEP and spent more time doing it than any previous President.

No less critical in his assessment of the President, a leading journalist, H. L. Mencken, wrote in the *American Mercury:* "He will be ranked among the vacuums. There is no principle in his armamentarium which is worthy of any sacrifice, even of sleep. There is no record that he ever thought anything worth hearing about any of the problems confronting him. His characteristic way of dealing with them is simply to avoid them, as a sensible man avoids an insurance solicitor or his wife's relatives."

BIG BUSINESS GAINS A FRIEND

The trusts and monopolies could not have found a better friend than Calvin Coolidge. The shackles that had been imposed on business to keep it fair and square were completely ripped off. All anti-trust prosecutions of any importance were stopped. Said the President: "We have got so many regulatory laws that I feel we would be better off if we did not have any more. . . . It does not at all follow that because abuses exist that it is the concern of the federal government to attempt their reform. . . ."

The Aluminum Company of America, controlled by Secretary of the Treasury Andrew W. Mellon and his family, and charged with operating a monopoly, was declared "not guilty" when it was threatened by a Congressional investigating committee.

The Federal Trade Commission, which had been brought into existence to investigate and enjoin illegal practices in interstate trade, was denounced by William E. Humphrey, an assistant of the President, as "an instrument of oppression and disturbance and injury instead of help to business." Prosecutions were hamstrung by a new rule that any information supplied by a company under investigation could not be turned over to the Department of Justice without the company's consent. There was to be no publicity about a company's violating a trade practice ruling until a final determination was made by the Commission.

When William Culbertson, the vice chairman of the United States Tariff Commission, endangered the sales and profits of America's giant industrialists by suggesting that tariffs on imported goods be reduced, Coolidge nicely got rid of the "thorn in the side of American industry" by appointing him ambassador to Rumania.

Observing all of this, another leading journalist, Lincoln Steffens, wrote: "Coolidge responded to the charge that government was a kept woman of business by marrying Wall Street to Washington, D.C."

A BAD TIME FOR LABOR

The National Association of Manufacturers, waging a remorseless, unabashed war against unionism, declared in 1925 that "the working classes hold to the right principles when they are left alone, but are unwittingly susceptible to excitement by agitating exploiters and professional uplifters. . . . The palatial temples of labor, whose golden domes rise in exultant splendor throughout the nation, the millions of dollars extracted by the jewelled hand of greed from the pockets of wage earners, and paid out in lucrative salaries to a ravenous band of pretenders, tell the pitiful story of a slavery such as this country has never known before."

Unable to cope with attacks such as this, the American Federation of Labor, the largest of the unions (the Congress of Industrial Organizations did not then exist), lost much of its prestige and power, and more than one million members. Adding further to organized labor's woes, the Supreme Court ruled that it was illegal for a union to attempt to organize workers who had agreed with an employer to reject unionism.

Strikes, which seldom took place during the Coolidge Administration, were frowned upon by most Americans, who saw them as "Socialist or radical plots," or as a cause of increased living costs. Except for a coal strike in 1923, there was no other serious labor trouble.

The power of labor unions against employers was not to be strengthened until 1935, when Congress passed the Wagner Act.

AARON SAPIRO VERSUS HENRY FORD

Aaron Sapiro, a Detroit lawyer and a leading figure in the farm cooperative movement, which Calvin Coolidge looked upon as a solution to the farmer's economic problem, sued Henry Ford, the president of the Ford Motor Company, for one million dollars, in 1927, for having libeled him and the Jewish race at large.

The *Dearborn* [Michigan] *Independent*, a newspaper controlled by Ford, had attacked Sapiro as one of a group of "Jewish bankers who seek to control the food markets of the world."

Ford, who was somewhat taken aback at Sapiro's
198

picking an Irish lawyer to represent him in the libel suit, came close to upsetting the court in the middle of the trial, by muttering, every now and then, that the "Catholics are tools of the Jews."

The judge, contending that Sapiro could not sue in behalf of an entire people and pocket the damages for himself, and suspecting that Ford had "bribed" a woman on the jury, declared a mistrial.

To the surprise of everybody, Ford made a public apology to all American Jews, closed down his newspaper, and paid for all of Sapiro's legal expenses, which reportedly amounted to $114,000.

But this did not end the Jewish boycott of Ford cars.

WHITES AGAINST BLACKS

Blacks found that life in the North, except for better jobs and wages, was about the same as it was in the South. They could no more buy or rent real estate in certain districts of Northern cities than they could in certain districts of Southern cities. No matter what part of the country they happened to be in, they could not get a room in a white man's hotel, buy a ticket to a white man's theatre, or eat in a white man's restaurant. Although the number of lynchings of blacks dropped from 86 in 1919 to only nine in 1929—largely because of the decline of the Ku Klux Klan—there was still plenty of other violence during this decade.

At Carteret, New Jersey, after a local prizefighter was stabbed to death by some blacks, a mob of white men, some dressed as Klansmen, burned to the ground the First Baptist Church, which had all black parishioners, and forced the parson, along with his wife and daughter, to leave town.

Near Marshall, Texas, a black farm laborer was whipped to death by several whites because he had cursed his white employer.

BLACK LYNCHING: A Missouri black, accused of attempting to assault a girl, was hanged without the benefit of a trial.

In Columbia, Missouri, while several hundred students of the University of Missouri looked on, a black accused of attempting to assault a 14-year-old girl was hanged, without the benefit of any sort of trial.

In September, 1929, the rector of an Episcopalian church in Brooklyn, New York, asked from his pulpit that the blacks sitting in his congregation leave immediately. "The Episcopal church provides churches for Negroes. Several of these churches are within easy reach of this locality." Journalist Heywood Broun expressed his indignation in his column in the *New York World:* "The reverend assumes that the Lord's house, which he tends, is one of the better country clubs. There is no record that Jesus Christ ever said, 'Suffer the little Caucasian children to come unto me.'"

AMERICA REBUFFS CANADA

America's refusal to recognize the interests and aspirations of Canada, her friendliest neighbor and best customer, was almost unbelievable. In 1929, shortly before Calvin Coolidge vacated the White House, the House of Representatives began to hold hearings preliminary to the hiking up of tariff schedules, for which there was no excuse in that prosperous period. The proposed prohibitory rates on goods imported from Canada gave rise to such a loud cry of anti-American feeling in the Canadian press, and to so many threats of retaliation, that William Phillips, America's ambassador to Canada, took the next train to Washington, D.C., at the request of William Lyon Mackenzie King, Canada's prime minister and leader of the Canadian Liberal party, to see if he could do anything about lessening the greed of the tax promoters. Phillips called on President-elect Herbert C. Hoover, believing that he, as a former Secretary of Commerce, would be best able to see that if the threatened high tariff against Canadian products became law, Canada's Conservative party would ride in on a wave of anti-American resentment. Hoover, showing no interest in the matter, referred the ambassador to the Congressional Ways and Means Committee, which consented to lend him an ear.

Phillips realized that the Committee knew nothing about Canadian geography, so he got hold of a map, intending to point out the location of Canadian provinces, and to illustrate his exposition of their interests and powers of retaliation. The ambassador, much to his surprise, was politely asked to leave, with the astonishing explanation that the Committee was not the least bit interested in exports from the United States, and cared only about keeping out imports.

A short time later, in 1930, Congress passed the Hawley-Smoot Tariff, imposing the highest taxes on imports in American history. Canada, of course, retaliated in kind; and, within a year, some 90 American manufacturers of automobiles, foods, pharmaceuticals, textiles, and other products circumvented the tariff problem by establishing branch factories in various Canadian provinces. The catastrophic drop in American exports to Canada did much to deepen the Great Depression, which followed in the wake of the stock market crash in 1929. Retaliatory tariffs, adopted by other nations that were as much upset by America's action as Canada was, caused a sharp decline in all American business overseas. It was not until 1933, when Franklin D. Roosevelt became President, that anything was done to lower the trade barrier.

30
THE GREAT
DEPRESSION

The Constitution of the United States, clearly stating that "no religious test shall be required of any candidate for the Presidency," was apparently completely ignored in the Presidential election of 1928, when Alfred E. Smith, a Democrat from New York, ran against Herbert C. Hoover, a Republican from California. Smith, a Catholic, did not have a chance of winning more votes than Hoover, a Protestant. The people, observing an old "rule" of American politics, would not choose a "Romanist" to occupy the White House, any more than they would choose a Jew. Ready, too, were they to believe ridiculous rumors, spread by the Ku Klux Klan, that there was a Catholic plot to take over the United States, and that, if elected, Smith would move the Pope from Rome to Washington, D.C. Try as he did to answer this scurrilous attack in his speeches, Smith got nowhere with the voters, even when he said that he believed in the "absolute separation of church and state," as specified in the Constitution.

Many lifelong Democrats, putting religion above politics, turned their backs on Smith and supported Hoover. During the next four years, according to

BANKS CLOSED TO
BUSINESS: Many of the
banks in the country,
including those of the
great financial center,
New York City, went
broke and closed their
doors when the stock
market crashed in 1929.

historian Andrew Sinclair, Hoover produced more
disaster than any other President.

CRASH GOES THE MARKET

Elected as the man who had managed to provide
food for starving Belgians in World War I, and as the
Secretary of Commerce who had managed to keep
America booming in the 1920's, Hoover now seemed
unable to prevent the Great Depression, arising from
the stock market crash of October, 1929, or to do anything to help poverty-stricken Americans. Banks failed
everywhere, while 13 million workers (out of a work
force of some 48 million) became jobless. Many families,
unable to pay rent or to meet mortgage payments, were
forced to live in hastily built packing-case shacks on city
dumps, ironically called "Hoovervilles." Breadlines
stretched from block to block in every city and town,

HOOVER ORDERED TROOPS AGAINST VETERANS when they appeared at the White House to demand payment of an overdue World War I service bonus.

while former executives were "downgraded" to selling apples on street corners. Some 20,000 army and navy veterans, marching to the nation's capital to demand payment of a long-overdue World War I service bonus, were roughed up on President Hoover's orders, and driven away from the White House by armed troops, led by General Douglas MacArthur and Colonel Dwight D. Eisenhower. A mutter of discontent rose to a cry for change, if not revolution.

DEPRESSION NOT RECOGNIZED

Nobody holding a top job in government or finance would admit that the stock market crash was a natural consequence of too much speculation, too much get-rich-quick production, and too much optimism; nor would Hoover and his aides even admit the existence of the

205

Great Depression, apparent as it was. The government's plan was to give business a shot in the arm through loans, to halt the decline in imports and exports, and to make European nations pay their debts, but nobody could decide on how to do it.

Incantation seemed to be the order of the day. The National Association of Manufacturers, made up of leading industrialists, dotted the nation with billboards, reading "Business is Good. Keep it Good. Nothing can stop the U.S.A." John D. Rockefeller, with millions of dollars rolling in from his Standard Oil Company, issued a statement to the press: "Fundamental conditions of the country are sound. . . . My son [John D., Jr.] and I are accumulating shares of stock." President Hoover, the leader of the exorcisers, told the people that "any lack of confidence in the basic strength of business is foolish. . . . Business and industry have turned the corner. . . . We have now passed the worst." On the other hand, his Secretary of the Treasury, Andrew W. Mellon, felt that it would be a good thing if employment, stocks, real estate, and everything else went right to the bottom: "People will work harder, and live a more moral life. Values will be adjusted, and enterprising people will pick up the wrecks from less competent people."

Hoover, reluctant to take any bold, imaginative steps, came up with too little, too late. Federal loans for business, relief for farmers, and plans for public works were all tried half-heartedly. He could not see that the total collapse of the American system of finance and world trade needed something more to give new life to the dying factories and farms. He vetoed a bill to give aid and federal jobs to millions of people, all because of his fear of unbalanced budgets and inflation.

SCHEMERS GET RICH

Hard times and all, many tycoons made money. One of them, a Chicagoan named Samuel E. Insull, became chairman of the directorates of 65 utility companies and wound up fleecing stockholders to the tune of $700 million. Indicted by a Cook County, Illinois, grand jury, he fled to Greece, and then to Turkey, where he was arrested and turned over to an American official. Brought back to Chicago, he was put on trial in a federal court, but allowed to go free when the judge ruled that there were no statutes that could be sufficiently applied to his case.

Equally crooked was Ivar Kreuger, the Swedish match king, who even went so far as to counterfeit Italian government bonds to deceive the auditors of his books. "Uncle Ivar," assuming a virtuous look and claiming to be a close friend of European bigwigs, was able to buy Diamond Match and a number of other American companies for a "song" and to employ the highly respected Boston banking firm of Lee, Higginson & Company as his representative in the United States. American investors, hoping to make a "fast buck," bought some $250 million of his worthless stock; even Harvard University had a substantial piece of it in its treasury when the match king, caught at last, committed suicide in 1932.

Another case was that of the United States & Foreign Securities Corporation, a holding company, incorporated under the laws of Maryland by Dillon, Read & Company, a New York City investment house, in which James V. Forrestal, a future Secretary of Defense, held a partnership. The holding company, able to control other businesses, had almost unlimited power to "purchase, hold, and deal with investment securities" and to "engage in commercial, manufacturing, and industrial enterprises." Dillon, Read absorbed 500,000 shares of

U.S. & F.S. common stock, while Forrestal took 37,000, of which he transferred some 20,000 to the Beekman Company Limited of Canada, a stock-juggling "ghost corporation," which was wholly controlled by the Beekman Corporation of Delaware, whose entire stock was owned by Forrestal and his wife. Beekman Limited sold more than 16,000 shares of U.S. & F.S. stock to the public at $53 a share. The stock, well promoted, rose to $72 just before the stock market crash in 1929, then dropped to less than $1.50 in 1932. There was much fancy trading and borrowing between the two Beekman corporations and Forrestal, who made a profit of nearly $900,000 for himself. The reason for such a complicated set-up, then considered legal, was to enable Forrestal to evade paying income or capital-gains taxes from the sale of his stock, which, in all, had cost him less than $29,000. Apparently bothered by his conscience, the "Wall Streeter" eventually paid a large sum in back taxes; but the "little fellows" who had bought the really worthless stock lost everything that they had.

TIME FOR A CHANGE

Hoover, the last of three successive Republican Presidents who believed in a government of the rich, by the rich, and for the rich, came close to presiding over the liquidation of the big moneymakers in America. It was a time when, as writer F. Scott Fitzgerald observed, the wealthy, greatly distrusted by other Americans, were only happy in each other's company. Ironically, they were to be saved from ruin by the man whom they denounced as a "traitor to his class"—Franklin D. Roosevelt, a wealthy Democrat from New York.

31
F.D.R.'S NEW DEAL

Most of the voters, fearing that the "American system" needed desperate measures to be saved, were more than willing to take a chance on the New Deal that Franklin D. Roosevelt promised to give them in return for their support in the Presidential election of 1932. His very presence and voice, spread far and wide by movie screens and radio, exuded confidence. Carrying all but six states, he polled almost 22.8 million votes against Herbert C. Hoover's 15.8. His huge victory, and the failure of the Socialists and Communists to poll more than a million votes, showed how strongly Americans still believed in free enterprise, despite its tremendous failure. The Democrats, trouncing the Republicans, elected emphatic majorities to both houses of Congress. There was never a stronger popular mandate in American history for a new program or policy, or a clearer repudiation of *laissez faire*. As humorist Will Rogers put it, "The little fellow felt that he never had a chance and he didn't till November the Eighth. And did he grab it!"

A RESHUFFLING OF THE CARDS

The New Deal, embracing both social and economic reforms, was not so much of a new game of cards as a reshuffling of the old American deck. Opponents saw it as near-Fascism or near-Communism, but it was as American as apple pie—the program of a dabbler in power, and of one ready to try anything to save capitalism. Aiming to offer something to everybody, Roosevelt acted at once to salvage private property as well as people, and banks as well as human bellies; but he remained conservative at the roots. His very first measure, the Emergency Banking Act of 1933, reopened the banks, then closed throughout the country, by immediately lending them a billion dollars instead of nationalizing them, as many people had expected him to do. Although new banking and stock market laws were passed to prevent the abuses which had allowed the fevered boom of the 1920's, banks and shares of stock were still left in the hands of the abusers. Roosevelt was merely shoring up a shattered system, and patching rather than reconstructing. Loans were made to home owners threatened with eviction because of their debts. Public housing projects were started, as were federal programs to bring electricity to the countryside. New government commissions went about regulating big business, since Roosevelt knew that it would not reform itself; as always, business was out to make more profits, not to create more jobs.

Workers fortunate enough to have jobs during the Great Depression that followed the stock market crash of 1929 were not much better off than those who had no work. Department stores, which had become notorious for low wages, paid clerks no more than $10 a week. Working women in Chicago labored for less than 25 cents an hour. Household servants received room and board and perhaps $10 a month. Secretaries in New York City worked for $15 a week. Codes of "fair practice," written for the big employers and big unions, did nothing to help small companies and unorganized unskilled workers, who found themselves being squeezed more than ever between the giant organizations of businessmen and unions of skilled workers. Some 200 large corporations, owning nearly half of the non-financial assets of American industry, looked to Roosevelt for protection against anti-trust laws, and got it. Farmers, receiving special consideration, were paid by the government for plowing under their surplus crops, in order to drive up farm prices. Upholding this principle, the government still sometimes pays farmers for not growing certain vegetables at certain times.

BLACKS GET THE SAME OLD DEAL

Blacks, disproportionately high on the lists of un-employed and disproportionately low on the lists of work relief, suffered far more than whites during the dismal days of the 1930's. The Civilian Conservation Corps (C.C.C.), set up by the President to carry out projects for the conservation of natural resources, enlisted only about 8 per cent of its total work force of 2.5 million from the ranks of young blacks. The new Works Progress Administration (W.P.A.), charged with starting public works to stem the rising tide of poverty and unemployment, did a little better, and, by January, 1935, blacks constituted about 30 per cent of its personnel. None too many black neighborhoods were helped by New Deal agencies building apartments, hospitals, and schools.

Although the New Deal was not marked by any official mandate from the White House to improve the lives of blacks, it did, strangely enough, have its effect in black communities, most of which shifted their loyalty from the Republican to the Democratic party. Even in the Presidential election of 1932, in the midst of the Great Depression, most blacks voted Republican. But by the election of 1936, black voting allegiance, to the extent

211

that colored people were allowed to vote at all, had switched largely to F.D.R. and the Democratic party. Very much against racial discrimination, the President's wife, Eleanor, won many more blacks over to the party's side in 1939, when she publicly denounced the Daughters of the American Revolution, an all-white patriotic society, for not allowing famed black singer Marian Anderson to give a concert in Constitution Hall, a "sacred edifice" of the Daughters in Washington, D.C.

The *New York Times*, noting that lynching had been declining steadily in the United States, reported on May 10, 1940, the startling statistic that the South had gone a whole year without hanging a black.

BRICKBATS FROM LEFT AND RIGHT

Franklin D. Roosevelt was as unpopular with the *right-wingers* as with the *left-wingers*. The Great Depression not only had given rise to demagogues and cranks, each with his own idea for a "cure-all," but also had a devastating effect on many young college graduates and jobless intellectuals. To them, representative government and capitalism were over and done with. Searching for something "new," some picked Fascism, while others picked Communism.

William D. Pelley, "the flower of our Protestant Christian manhood," organized the Silver Shirts, who imitated Adolf Hitler's Storm Troopers by terrorizing Jews and Liberals.

Lawrence Dennis, a graduate of Harvard and conscience-stricken New York City banker, turned toward the German dictator as a new god.

The Reverend Gerald L. K. Smith, the head of the America First party, along with the Reverend Charles E. Coughlin, the operator of the "Shrine of the Little Flower Radio Station," pointed an accusing finger at F.D.R., contending that he was Jewish, that his real name was Rosenfeld, and that his New Deal was actually a "Jew Deal."

Ridiculous as all of this was, it still got some measure of support from newspaper publisher William Randolph Hearst, who had visited Hitler and liked him. An untold number of college students, touring Germany during the Great Depression, watched the Hitler Youth marching, singing, and "doing their thing," and, upon returning home to find nothing but apathy, discontent, and unemployment, became Nazi converts.

Many financiers felt that Roosevelt posed a serious threat to big business, and, in such a respectable magazine as *Fortune*, Laird S. Goldsborough, the foreign editor of *Time*, its sister publication, wrote: "The good journalist must recognize in Fascism certain ancient virtues of the race, whether or not they happen to be momentarily fashionable in his own country. Among these are Discipline, Duty, Courage, Glory, and Sacrifice."

Although the American Fascist movement never really got anywhere, it did attract many people who turned traitor to the United States during World War II, including such notables as poet Ezra Pound, who broadcast Fascist propaganda for Italy's dictator, Benito Mussolini; and Hearst newspaperman Fred Kaltenbach, who served Hitler in a like capacity.

THE "REDS"

On the opposite side of the fence was the American Communist party, headed by Earl Browder, who, obeying his boss, Joseph Stalin in Moscow, ordered the membership "to liquidate every old idea that stands as an obstacle between us and the masses." The *New York Daily Worker*, the party's official publication in the United States, attacked Franklin D. Roosevelt as a "covert Fascist," and the New Deal as the "death rattle of capitalism." Featherbrained labor-union leaders—

particularly those of the Chicago meat packers—got the bright idea that they "could use the Commies," and encouraged them to join their organization, only to discover that they were the ones who were being used. The National Maritime Union, making the same mistake, wound up by threatening the entire structure of national defense by holding up the shipment of war materiel to France in 1940, but quickly changed its tune and became patriotic when Hitler decided to attack Russia in 1941.

Besides worming their way into labor unions, the Communists also took over the National Negro Congress, organized by anti-Reds such as Ralph Bunche; the American Student Union, which claimed 20,000 members; and the American Youth Congress, made up largely of zealous Liberals.

Promising an ideal form of society and offering a gospel of all-embracing love for mankind, Communism appealed to many American intellectuals, who were convinced that *this*, not Fascism, was "the wave of the future." Greatly disturbed by German atrocities, they completely overlooked the Russian purges and executions.

Impressed by what Communism seemed to offer, many up-and-coming young men—such as Whittaker Chambers, an editor of *Time*; and Alger Hiss, a brilliant lawyer—sought and got jobs in the federal government. Upon the establishment of a "Red cell" in the nation's capital, the *left-wingers* met regularly and laughed their heads off over Roosevelt's efforts to put the broken-down capitalistic system back together again. A few of them stole government documents, which they hurriedly sent off to Russia. Looking forward to the day of the "great revolution," they confidently expected to be made commissars of the "American Soviet Federated Socialist Republic," just as Hitler's supporters confidently expected to enjoy similar recognition when Germany put America on her back. But, much to their disappointment, the American Communist party was shortly "policed" out of significance.

THE "LIBERTY LEAGUERS"

There were also other groups of angry plotters, each with some sort of wild scheme; but no one of them was ever so formidable as the American Liberty League, a big-business cabal, which cooked up one of the most reprehensible conspiracies in American history. Perhaps because the plan misfired, or because it involved the associates of such prominent American families as the Du Ponts, Morgans, and Rockefellers—plus two former Democratic Presidential candidates, John W. Davis and Alfred E. Smith—the whole affair was almost completely ignored by the press. But for Jules Archer's exposing it in *The Plot to Seize the White House*, the incident might never have been brought to light.

It all began in 1933, when two American Legionnaires, representing the American Liberty League, approached Smedley Darlington Butler, a retired Marine general, offering him some $3 million to mobilize an army of 500,000 veterans, and march them to the nation's capital, where they were to depose the President, and install a dictator to take over the government of the United States. The League, determined to put an end to the "socialism" of the Roosevelt Administration and to bring about a return to the doctrines of a *laissez-faire* economy, sent out reams of propaganda, and even had a man touring Europe to study the success that the Fascists had had with certain veterans' organizations.

Butler, twice a winner of the Congressional Medal of Honor and a hero in the eyes of American veterans, seemed a likely candidate for the dictatorship. But he

215

reported the plot in detail to the House Un-American Activities Committee, then chaired by Congressman John W. McCormack of Massachusetts, later Speaker of the House. At the hearings, the go-betweens denied everything, and the Committee was simply afraid to subpoena as witnesses the tycoons of industry and finance who were allegedly implicated in the plot. Another problem was that the whole plan seemed too preposterous to be taken seriously. And it was never decided whether the supporters of the American Liberty League knew about what was really going on. The League was finally disbanded in 1936. But author Archer had every reason to believe that the plot was in earnest, as did Congressman McCormack, who once told him: "They were going to make it all sound constitutional, of course, with a high-sounding name for the dictator, and a plan to make it all sound like a good American program."

THE CATHOLIC LOBBY

The Catholics, although a political as well as a numerical minority, conducted the most powerful religious lobby on Capitol Hill and did not hesitate to ask Congressmen for favors in return for their political support. President Roosevelt, influenced by the Catholic bloc, permitted the church to censor American magazines; and, in foreign affairs, he applied an embargo against arms to Spain so that the Catholic hierarchy could help the Fascist government, even when he knew that the European democracies were about to have a showdown with the European dictators.

Postmaster General Frank Walker, a Catholic, all but surrendered to Bishop John F. Noll of Fort Wayne, Indiana, the power to deny second-class mailing privileges to magazines that offended the National Organization for Decent Literature by featuring crime,

CATHOLICS
CENSORED
MAGAZINES and
exercised tight control
over publications read
by all religious groups.

sex, and violence. A letter, written by William Smith, the head of the N.O.D.L. office in Washington, D.C., amply illustrated how tight Catholic control was over magazines read by all religious groups:

Your Excellency:

During the past week, Mr. Selinka, counsel for the Dell Publishing Company, brought to me a revised dummy of *Modern Romance* magazine. Since they made the changes which I suggested . . . this magazine does not violate the code.

Mr. William H. Fawcett, accompanied by the new editorial director of their confession magazines, Mr. William H. Lingel, called on me with the dummy of *Romantic Story*. I carefully read this dummy and made a few minor changes in it, but had to object to one of the stories. Mr. Lingel assured me that this story . . . would be changed . . .

I talked to Mr. Hassel, counsel in the solicitor's office of the Post Office Department. He told me that the following magazines had been cited for hearings to show cause why their second-class mailing privileges should not be revoked. They are: *Special Detective Cases, Romantic Story,* and *Crime Confession.* I shall, of course, attend these hearings.

The Post Office Department is apparently trying to avoid as much publicity as possible with regard to these hearings, because no news releases were sent out naming the magazines or giving the dates and times of the hearings.

Most respectfully yours,
William Smith

Thomas G. Corcoran, a close friend and adviser to Franklin D. Roosevelt, in agreement with Catholic reactionaries in the United States, worked effectively at the White House to keep the embargo on all American weapons to both sides in the Spanish Civil War—a move that had the effect of denying American guns and tanks to the Spanish Loyalist government, while in no way preventing the flow of German and Italian guns and tanks to General Francisco Franco, the leader of the insurgents. Helped this way, the Spanish Fascists won the war in 1939, and Franco assumed the powers of a dictator. Roosevelt, no longer concerned about Spain, and informed of Hitler's march into Poland, directed his attention to the protection of England and France. The embargo against arms to European nations was lifted, enabling the democracies to buy the American goods that they so badly needed.

R.C.A. GETS ITS WAY

The case of the Radio Corporation of America, one of the biggest anti-trust suits in American history, dated back to the closing days of the Hoover Administration, when the Department of Justice tried to break up the radio trust that the giant military-industrial complex had created by working out deals with American

218

Telephone and Telegraph, General Electric, and Westinghouse.

Not wanting to go to court and run the risk of getting bad publicity, R.C.A. managed to obtain postponement after postponement until Department of Justice counsel Warren Olney refused to accept any further delays. With the trial date set for October, 1932, David Sarnoff, the chairman of R.C.A. and later a brigadier general in World War II, confided to his attorney that he was certain that his good friend Roosevelt would win the forthcoming Presidential election. The company chairman, who made a practice of "buying" both Republican and Democratic Congressmen for the benefit of R.C.A., paid out $7,500 to Senator Dan Hastings of Delaware—the state in which the case was to be tried—to get Henry C. Mahaffy, the clerk of the United States District Court in Wilmington, to arrange for a postponement. Mahaffy, unable to resist $2,500 in cash from R.C.A. (some said that it was $25,000), got Judge John J. Nields to say that he was "indisposed," and that the trial would have to be postponed. The judge, afraid that he might be impeached, retired, as did the clerk of the court. The trial, seemingly forgotten by the Department of Justice after Roosevelt's winning the Presidency, never took place.

F.D.R. BREAKS HIS PROMISE

The fall of France, Italy's decision to become an ally of Germany, and the "battle of Britain," which all took place in 1940, led to a change in the American neutralist attitude toward World War II. Neutrality laws were repealed. Roosevelt, forgetting his 1940-election promise that American boys would not be sent into any foreign war, and declaring that America was the "arsenal of democracy," gave aid to England. By the Lend-Lease Act of 1941, $7 billion was loaned to the British to buy

219

war materiel from the United States. American destroyers went into action against German submarines in the Atlantic. When Germany invaded Russia in 1941, $6 billion in Lend-Lease went to the Russians.

AMERICA UNPREPARED FOR WAR

Great Britain warned the United States to prepare for a Japanese attack in the Pacific, but even when the American military establishment knew that a bombing of one of America's possessions (Hawaii or the Philippines) was imminent, it yet remained unprepared. With Germany keeping Russia busy defending her western front, Japan had no cause to worry about a Russian attack through Manchuria. Roosevelt's embargo on the export of oil, iron, and steel to Japan, was supposed to prevent her total victory over China, but it proved to be more of an irritant than a deterrent. So did his insistence that Japan withdraw from China and Indochina, and that a peace settlement be worked out to cover the entire Pacific. Instead, Japan decided to ally herself with Germany and Italy, and, at dawn, on December 7, 1941, attacked Pearl Harbor, inflicting a humiliating defeat on the sleeping Army and Navy there. Congress immediately declared war on Japan, while Germany and Italy declared war on the United States.

With industrialists landing profitable defense contracts, and with jobless workers landing jobs and earning more money than they had ever earned in their lives, the economic situation in the United States took on a new look.

THE DRAWING OF THE COLOR LINE

The same color line that had been drawn in World War I was again drawn in World War II. The United States Marines and the Coast Guard accepted only whites. The Army and the Air Corps separated blacks from whites, while the Navy signed them up for nothing but menial tasks. It was not until 1940 that blacks were allowed to attend white schools for the training of officers. Roosevelt's "Four Freedoms," for which America presumably went to war—freedom of speech, freedom of religion, freedom from want, and freedom from fear— were still for white Americans only.

AMERICA'S CONCENTRATION CAMPS

Some 30,000 Japanese-Americans had just cause to wonder why they had been so willing to volunteer for combat in the Army of the United States. Their families, most of whom lived in Hawaii, California, Oregon, and Washington, had their bank accounts "frozen" by the

JAPANESE-AMERICANS TREATED LIKE ENEMIES: The families of Japanese-Americans who provided the Army of the United States with two of its finest fighting forces in Europe were forced to live in concentration camps in the United States.

federal government shortly after Pearl Harbor. By the end of 1942, F.D.R. and the federal government had all of them living in concentration camps. Victimized by their lily-white neighbors, who were quick to take advantage of their "enemy status," American-born Japanese were forced to take but a few hundred dollars for their cars; a few thousand for their stores with everything in them; a tenth of their value for homes, farms, or fishing boats. Roosevelt, while condemning Hitler's inhumanity to Jews, gave no thought to his own inhumanity to Japanese-Americans.

Telling the ugly story in *Americans Betrayed*, author Morton Grodzin wrote:

> One hundred ten thousand Americans of Japanese ancestry were evacuated. Aliens and citizens, children and adults, and male and female were moved on short notice from their lifetime homes to concentration centers. No charges were ever filed against these persons and no guilt ever attributed to them. The test was ancestry applied with the greatest rigidity. Evacuation swept into guarded camps orphans, foster-children in white homes, Japanese married to Caucasians, the off-spring of Japanese ancestry, and American citizens with as little as one-sixteenth Japanese blood. Evacuation was not carried out by lawless vigilantes or by excited local officials. The program was instituted and executed by military forces of the U.S., with a full mandate of power from both the Executive and the Legislative branches of the national government.

Overlooking the unfair treatment of their families, the *Nisei* (American-born Japanese) provided two of the finest fighting forces in the Army of the United States— the 100th Infantry Battalion and the 442nd Regimental

222

FRANKLIN CHEATED ON ELEANOR: The President preferred a mistress to a wife when it came to sex.

Combat Team. Proving their loyalty to the Stars and Stripes, they fought their way from southern Italy to northern Germany. With 60 per cent of their number wounded or killed in action, they proved how unwise it was to compel other Japanese-Americans to remain in concentration camps.

THE UNTOLD STORY

As even the most casual reader of Rooseveltiana knows, the life of Eleanor Roosevelt was filled with trouble and woe. Her father, an alcoholic, died young, and her mother and brother were claimed by an early death as well. Her marriage to her cousin Franklin seemed a lucky break, but mother-in-law Sara Delano Roosevelt turned out to be a meddlesome tyrant, and F.D.R. himself had plenty of weaknesses as a husband. As narrated by his son Elliott in *An Untold Story: The Roosevelts of Hyde Park*, all five of F.D.R.'s children heard about his love affair with Lucy Mercer and knew about her successor in the boudoir, Missy LeHand.

Eleanor, acquiescing to an amazing degree, treated her husband's mistress as a daughter, and even shopped for her. The faithful wife, according to Elliott, took no pleasure in sex, while F.D.R., on the other hand,

223

matured into a lusty, sexy fellow, whose interest and prowess in lovemaking were undiminished, even by the after-effects of polio. Lonely and hurt by Franklin's indifference in the 1920's, Eleanor began an assortment of good works and political activities (the latter for F.D.R.'s benefit).

In the eyes of Elliott, she was by no means the self-sacrificing, praiseworthy woman that many historians have said she was. A poor housekeeper, she did not feed the children as well as Granny Sara did. To get in the good graces of the bigoted Sara, Eleanor often feigned anti-Semitic ideas. Some years later, as an author, syndicated newspaper columnist, and magazine writer, she had the boldness to picture herself as a "calm, contented woman" rather than as the "detached, harried, faultfinding wife and parent we knew." To daughter Anna, she was insensitive, and "poor company on a camping trip."

Roosevelt should never have run for a fourth term in 1944. (Only after 1951 did an Amendment to the Constitution prevent a President from being elected more than twice.) But, above all else, F.D.R. wanted another victory, so that he, not the Republican candidate, Thomas E. Dewey of New York, would be the one to "finish off the war," and bring about the peace. Had his physicians told the truth and reported him as "tired and sick" instead of lying about his being "fit as a fiddle," the Democrats would have undoubtedly picked another candidate. Roosevelt, tired of the left-wing vagaries of Henry A. Wallace, his third-term Vice President, dumped him and picked Harry S. Truman, a little-known machine politician and Senator from Missouri, as his running mate. Less than three months after his inauguration on January 20, 1945, Roosevelt died of a cerebral hemorrhage, and Truman took his place.

32

THE TRUMAN
SCANDALS

President Harry S. Truman, the product of one of the
most corrupt political machines in American history—
the Pendergast machine of Kansas City—surrounded
himself with mediocre Democratic cronies who did
nothing but clutter his Administration with scandals.
Strong Chief Executive though he was at a critical time
in history, Truman made a number of mistakes that
could have been politically fatal. Among these were the
hurried demobilization of American armed forces
following the conclusion of World War II; insistence
on continuing meat rationing after the wartime spirit of
sacrifice had run its course; and failure to get Congressional approval for taking the United States into the
Korean War. The Truman Fair Deal program, consisting largely of a continuation and development of the
principles of Franklin D. Roosevelt's New Deal, failed
to bring about any advances in civil rights. True, the
so-called Truman Doctrine led to the rebuilding of
Europe on American money, and to the containment of
Communism across the globe by American aid and arms.
But Communist successes in China and eastern Europe
made America's suspicion of China and Russia grow into

fear—and when that fear swelled into hysteria, Truman was forced to purge the government of many suspected Communist sympathizers.

TRUMAN'S CRONIES

There was scarcely a month when some Congressional committee did not have a just cause for grilling one of President Truman's friends for some peccadillo or outright misfeasance. Convicted criminals who had "good connections" were getting hasty pardons, while influential officeholders were being loaded with favors and bribes. Lobbyists, operating as "fixers" and "influence peddlers," were making money hand over fist by offering clients ways to get government loans and contracts, dodge taxes, and cut red tape.

Leading a Congressional investigation of all this hanky-panky, Senator J. William Fulbright of Arkansas discovered that General Harry L. Vaughan, a poker-playing pal of Truman and his military aide, had done favors for perfume smugglers and accepted deep freezers as gifts, and that the wife of E. Merle Young, an official of the Reconstruction Finance Corporation (R.F.C.), had received a $10,000 mink coat after he had approved a government loan to a Florida motel. Vaughan continued to remain in the President's good graces, while Young got off easy with a short jail sentence.

Mayor James M. Curley of Boston, a prince of demagogues, was convicted of mail fraud and sent to prison, but Truman used his constitutional power and granted him a pardon.

Four members of the Al Capone gang—Louis "Little New York" Campagna, Paul "the Waiter" DeLucia, Philip D'Andrea, and Charles "Cherry Nose" Gioe, had been sentenced to 10 years in prison for conspiracy to extort a million dollars from the movie industry. But they were all paroled in August, 1947, after having served only three-and-one-half years of their 10-year terms, and after having agreed to "deliver" a block of votes.

Mayor William O'Dwyer of New York City, who had no qualms about associating with gangsters and accepting money from questionable sources, escaped an investigation in 1950 by getting Truman to appoint him as America's ambassador to Mexico.

Another investigation, led by Congressman Cecil R. King of California, uncovered cases of "fixing" in the Internal Revenue Service and the Department of Justice. An assistant attorney general and the President's appointments secretary were convicted and sent to jail on conspiracy charges, as was a former I.R.S. commissioner, for tax evasion.

Truman, all too complacent about these goings on, eventually did some housecleaning in the Internal Revenue Service and the Department of Justice, and reorganized the Reconstruction Finance Corporation. But the deep freezers and the mink coat continued to plague him throughout the remainder of his Administration.

INDIANS LOSE THEIR LANDS

The American Indians, too poor to improve their lives without outside help, suffered during World War II, when the federal government, while spending billions of dollars to "save the world for democracy," told them that they would have to shift for themselves. Oil companies, deprived of foreign supplies, had discovered huge deposits of oil and other resources on some Indian reservations, and had gotten Congress to terminate the Indians' rights to this valuable real estate.

Shocked by the loss of their farms and grazing lands, the Hopi Indians of Arizona got their chiefs to write President Truman a letter, in which they not only summarized their case, but also pointed out that the

United States was behaving more like their enemy than their friend.

This land is the sacred home of the Hopi people. . . . We are still a sovereign nation. . . . We have never given up our sovereignty to any foreign power or nation. We were a self-governing people long before any white man came to our shores. Are you ever going to be satisfied with all the wealth you have now because of us, the Indians? There is something terribly wrong with your system of government, because after all these years, we, the Indians, are still licking on the bones . . . that fall to us from your tables. Have the American people, white people, forgotten the treaties with the Indians?

All the laws under the Constitution of the United States were made without our consent, knowledge, and approval, yet we are being forced to accept them.

The termination policy, which was officialized by Truman, put an end to the self-government of the Indian tribes. Federal aid to the Indians was discontinued. State governments were given the power to rule over the Indians within their boundaries. White corporations, playing footsie with state politicians, gained control of the resources on the Indian reservations.

The Klamath Indians of Oregon, who had long protected the great forests on their reservation, were forced to surrender their property rights to private lumber companies, which cut the trees and destroyed the woodlands. Like other tribes, the Klamath received little or nothing from the use of their acreage. There were long and expensive lawsuits, but, invariably, the Indians lost out.

Aiming to break up and "Americanize" the tribes,

the Bureau of Indian Affairs of the Department of the Interior sent thousands of Indian families to the cities, where most of them, lacking special skills and education, became part of the unemployed poor, living on welfare aid.

INFLATION CAUSES LABOR TROUBLES

Truman was unable to do anything about rising prices. The cattlemen and meat packers asked that price controls be lifted off beef when World War II ended, so that everyone could afford to eat steak. But when the legal limit was removed in 1946, beef sky-rocketed from 50 cents to over a dollar a pound. Eight basic commodities, including wheat, rose 25 per cent, while salaries dropped 12 per cent.

Labor unions, up in arms over all of this, ordered strikes across the nation, calling for wage increases in a number of industries. John L. Lewis, the head of the United Mine Workers, defied both the President and the courts by threatening a coal strike, and got away with it. The strike of the Railway Brotherhood, heretofore a responsible and respectable union, threatened to tie up the nation's entire transportation system—but Truman put an end to that by announcing that he would call in the Army to run the railroads.

The arrogance and public-be-damned attitude of the labor leaders gave rise to a hatred of unionism, which was reflected in the Congressional elections of 1946. The Republicans, who had been standing out in the cold for 15 years, drove most of the Democrats out of both houses of Congress. They also managed to push through the Taft-Hartley Act, which outlawed the closed shop, made unions liable for damages caused by a breach of contract, required a 60-day "cooling-off" period before a strike, forbade unions to make political contributions or to collect exorbitant dues from members,

229

and compelled elected union officers to swear that they were not Communists. The new law also worked to get the Reds out of the unions (unfortunately, not the criminal element as well), and to force labor leaders, with a few exceptions, to be more circumspect and less greedy. But comprehensive as the law was, it did not prevent labor unions from excluding blacks, Puerto Ricans, and other minorities from membership. As revealed by the National Association for the Advancement of Colored People (N.A.A.C.P.), there were no blacks among the electrical workers, plumbers, pipe fitters, sheet metal workers, bricklayers, painters, tile layers, and common laborers.

THE SECRET OIL DEAL

The Treasury Department, at the urging of the Department of State, gave way to a secret Cabinet-level decision in the summer of 1950, resulting in the establishment of a system by which international oil corporations would call their foreign *royalty payments* to oil-producing governments in the Middle East *tax payments* instead, and reduce their income-tax payments to the United States government correspondingly.

Wall Street lawyers were sent to the Middle East to help Saudi Arabia and neighboring nations rewrite their laws to bring them within the purview of the tax credit provisions of the United States Internal Revenue Code. The result of this arrangement was not revealed until Congress conducted an investigation in 1974.

The action, described by Senator Frank Church of Idaho as "the brainchild of the National Security Council," was carried out in "secret session" and "never legislated." According to the Senator, it was made "to insure stable, pro-United States governments in the oil producing countries of the Middle East."

Statistics, made public during the investigation,

showed that the Arabian American Oil Corporation, for example, paid United States taxes of $50 million in 1950, but only $6 million in 1951. Saudi Arabia, enjoying a gain of $44 million in tax revenue, collected $66 million from the company in 1950, and $110 million in 1951.

Other international oil corporations, including Standard Oil, Texaco, and Gulf, made billions of dollars abroad, but paid practically no taxes to the United States.

THE WITCH HUNT

The discovery that certain people in the United States had stolen atomic secrets for the Russians engendered a mania for persecution that resulted in one of the worst witch hunts in American history. Employers fired and blacklisted employees who were accused, without proof, of being Communists. Guilt was established by smear, and loss of job followed on a false witness.

Alger Hiss, formerly a man of some importance in the Department of State, was charged with perjury in denying to a federal grand jury that he had ever given confidential government documents to Whittaker Chambers, formerly an editor of *Time* magazine and an alleged Communist. After one jury disagreed, another found Hiss guilty, and he was sentenced to five years in a penitentiary.

Sometime later, in 1951, two New Yorkers, Julius and Ethel Rosenberg, were sentenced to death for having passed data on the atomic bomb to Russian agents. Eleven top Communists, found guilty of conspiracy to overthrow the government, were sent to jail.

AMERICA GOES TO WAR AGAIN

North Korea, staging an all-out attack against South Korea on June 25, 1950, had not thought that the United States would consider South Korea necessary for the defense of the Pacific, so she was caught by surprise when President Truman ordered the American Army and Navy to help the South Koreans, within 24 hours after the Korean War began. The lucky absence of Russia from the Security Council of the United Nations had allowed America's intervention in Korea as a member of the United Nations, since the North Koreans were condemned as aggressors. The war itself stimulated America's flagging economy, and, despite a see-saw campaign and massive Chinese intervention, the fighting resulted in a stalemate. General Douglas MacArthur, leading the forces of the United Nations, tried to get Truman to blockade China and bomb her cities. When the President ignored his advice, for fear of provoking another World War, the general wrote to Republicans in Congress that an open conflict with China was necessary. "By this act," Truman later said, "MacArthur left me no choice . . . I could no longer tolerate his insubordination." So Truman fired him, and ordered General Matthew B. Ridgway to take his place.

Then, what a blow up! Super-patriots half-masted American flags. Senator Richard M. Nixon of California demanded MacArthur's re-instatement, while Senator Joseph R. McCarthy of Wisconsin denounced the President as "a son of a bitch who decided to remove MacArthur when drunk." A Gallup Poll showed that the public favored the general against Truman 69 to 29. MacArthur, returning to the United States, received enthusiastic greetings from Republican Congressmen, and drew tears from television viewers when he quoted the Army ballad, "Old Soldiers Never Die, They Just Fade Away." But fade away, he did.

SENATORS STOOD UP FOR GENERAL: Senator Richard M. Nixon joined his friend Senator Joseph R. McCarthy in supporting MacArthur, and denouncing Truman when he fired the general.

TRUMAN SEIZES THE STEEL MILLS

Truman gave his constitutional powers a dangerous and unnecessary stretching in April, 1952, when he took sides with organized labor and seized the steel industry in the midst of an industrial dispute. The United Steelworkers' Union, at odds with the steel companies over wages and working conditions, had gotten nowhere in its arguments with management, and, at the request of the President, agreed to have the government's Wage Stabilization Board put a panel of labor experts on the case. The Board, favoring the steelworkers, handed down a wage recommendation that was acceptable to the steel union but not to the steel industry. Denouncing the steelmakers as "greedy," and ridiculing their argument for a price boost to cover increased operating costs, Truman seized the steel mills to prevent a strike, which the government's own generosity with the union had made inevitable.

United States District Judge David A. Pine, holding court in the nation's capital, ruled that the President's seizing of the steel industry was "illegal and without the authority of the law."

233

There is no express grant of power in the Constitution authorizing the President to direct this seizure. There is no grant of power from which it can reasonably be implied. There is no enactment of Congress authorizing it. No constitutional provisions grant the President . . . the power . . . to take such action.

The steel industry was returned to its owners, and the steel union called off the strike.

TRUMAN REFUSES TO RUN

Seeing how the wind was blowing with scandals about deep freezers and a mink coat still floating in the air, Truman announced that he would not try for a third term in the Presidential election of 1952. The Democrats, more than pleased by his decision, picked Governor Adlai Stevenson of Illinois, a man of passionate integrity, as their candidate. Skilled in government administration and filled with constructive ideas on domestic and foreign policies, he attracted the support of professors and other intellectuals, but his speeches were too "egghead" and scholarly to capture the votes of the general public. Unable to defend Truman's record, which had been badly marred by scandals, inflation, and discontent resulting from the Korean War, the Illinoian fought a loser's campaign.

33
"IKE" AND "DICK"

The Republicans, out of favor with many minorities and unionists in the election year of 1952, picked General Dwight D. Eisenhower, who had never lost a battle in World War II, as the one man in the United States almost certain to succeed to the White House—traditionally, the pension plan for America's military heroes. Although he was by no means the brilliant speaker that his Democratic opponent, Adlai E. Stevenson, was, Eisenhower did manage to make speeches that made him seem "pretty much for mother, home, and heaven." Making much of the peace theme that usually wins American elections, the general said that he himself would "go to Korea to seek an early and honorable end to the Korean War." Moreover, he seemed to offer exactly the right combination of "iron fist and velvet glove" to an electorate that blamed the Democrats for being too soft on Communists at home, and too hard overseas. Largely influenced by Eisenhower's pleasing personality and winning smile, most Americans voted for him with all the confidence that they would have in a favorite uncle. But a vote for "Ike" was also a vote for his running mate, Richard M.

Nixon, an aggressive politician and United States Senator from California, who was so evasive that he was accused of being the only man able to campaign in heaven and hell, and carry both places.

NIXON'S "SECRET FUND"

Without question, the high dramatic moment of the 1952 Presidential campaign came a little over a month before Election Day, when the *New York Post* revealed that a group of favor-seeking California millionaires had established a "secret fund" of $18,000 to help pay Richard M. Nixon's "personal expenses" as a Senator.

The contributors of the fund, according to the *Post*, had had heavy stakes in legislation on which Senator Nixon had voted. On issues of concern to the bankers, oilmen, real estate executives, government contractors, and others who contributed to his fund, the Senator voted their way right down the line. For example, he saved the oilmen millions of dollars in taxes by voting against reducing the $27\frac{1}{2}$ per cent oil depletion allowance, and pleased the real estate men by voting to reduce the availability of public housing, and hasten the end of wartime rent controls. Dana C. Smith, a friend of Nixon, who collected the fund, said "the contributors felt that Dick made a fine salesman for free enterprise, and that they believed he needed extra money to do the selling job."

Nixon, under heavy pressure to resign as the Republican candidate for Vice President, and threatened by a requirement from Eisenhower that he be "as clean as a hound's tooth," saved his political career by delivering his famous "Checkers" speech over nationwide television. What he did in that speech was to recite his life story; to tell of the struggles he had had; to say that his wife, Pat, could afford only a cloth coat, and not a mink coat; to charge that the "Communists and crooks"

236

were "smearing" him; and to claim that he had used the fund for political rather than personal expenses.

The Senator did not emerge as clean as a hound's tooth, but he did emerge as a skillful politician with enormous support from rank-and-file Republicans, and that turned out to be enough for Eisenhower. Both the "hound" and his "tooth" were soon forgotten. Dick was elected along with Ike.

THE WITCH HUNT GOES ON

Continuing the Red-baiting that had been going on in the House Un-American Activities Committee since 1950, Senator Joseph R. McCarthy of Wisconsin declared that the Democrats, led by Franklin D. Roosevelt and Harry S. Truman, had "conspired" to deliver the United States to the Communists. According to the Senator, it was F.D.R. who got America into World War II to help Russia, and H.S.T. who gave China to the Reds, and lost the Korean War. None the less guilty in the Wisconsinite's eyes were Secretary of State Dean Acheson, who hired hundreds of "known Communists" for the Department of State, and Secretary of Defense George C. Marshall, who tolerated a "gigantic Communist conspiracy" in the Department of Defense. There were, as claimed by McCarthy, Alger Hisses "concealed" in government offices, public schools, and corporations, who stood ready to "take over the United States" whenever Russian Premier Joseph Stalin pushed the button. Preposterous as all of this was, almost half the people in the nation believed it—for a while. Thousands of patriotic Americans, whose only crime was to have lent their names to some "Communist-front organization" prior to, or in the course of, World War II, lost their jobs as well as their reputations.

But for the spectacular demagoguery of Senator McCarthy and the mass hysteria generated by the

House Un-American Activities Committee, the idea of a "Communist conspiracy" would not have become as popular as it did. Estimates of the Senator and his objectives have varied from outright admiration to outright condemnation. Severely censured by the Senate in 1954, and subsequently rated by historians as "one of the biggest liars ever to enter politics," Joe McCarthy finally disappeared from the public scene.

TRUMAN SPEAKS HIS MIND

Harry S. Truman, expressing blunt thoughts about Eisenhower during an interview for Merle Miller's book *Plain Speaking*, claimed that Ike was a "weak" commander in World War II, and that later he was a "coward" for not squelching McCarthy's witch hunt for "Reds" in the government. But what really ticked the former President off was a letter that he said Ike had written to General George C. Marshall, the Army's chief of staff, after the war, asking to be relieved of duty so that he could divorce his wife, Mamie, and marry Kay Summersby, a member of the Women's Army Auxiliary Corps, who doubled as his chauffeur and secretary during the European campaign.

"Well," said Truman, "Marshall wrote him back a letter the like of which I never did see. He said that if Eisenhower ever came close to doing such a thing, he'd not only bust him out of the Army, he'd see to it that never for the rest of his life would he be able to draw a peaceful breath."

Truman then added: "I don't like Eisenhower. I never have, but one of the last things I did as President, I got those letters from his file in the Pentagon, and I destroyed them."

Admitting his hatred of Nixon, Truman said: "Nixon is a shifty-eyed goddamn liar, and the people know it."

IKE WAS A LOVER: The general wanted to divorce his wife, and marry his Army chauffeur and secretary.

DIRTY WORK IN THE CABINET

Constitutionally, there is no such thing as "the President's Cabinet." There are only heads of departments, and it depends on the Chief Executive what and how much influence a Cabinet member has. Eisenhower, who disliked having to make decisions and assume responsibilities, chose an advisory group, headed by Sherman Adams, to help him select his Cabinet. The President subsequently had cause to regret the confidence that he placed in Adams, and in certain Cabinet members.

Adams, who became almost indispensable to Eisenhower as his "deputy President," unfortunately intervened with the Federal Trade Commission and the Securities and Exchange Commission on behalf of a shady manipulator and income tax evader named Bernard Goldfine, from whom he received relatively expensive gifts and hospitality. When this came out, the President had to ask Adams for his resignation, suggesting that he return to New Hampshire and raise chickens.

John Foster Dulles, a lawyer and consultant on foreign affairs in the Truman Administration, whom Ike picked as his Secretary of State, gravely damaged the morale of his department by cowardly catering to

239

Senator McCarthy, and allowing him to force the resignation of loyal foreign service officers, "suspected" of being "soft on Communism."

Robert B. Anderson, a Texas financier, who was appointed as Ike's second-term Secretary of the Treasury, made himself close to $300,000 by doing a "favor" for some oilmen, just before the Senate confirmed his appointment. The President so greatly admired the Texan that he had wanted him to replace Nixon as his running mate in the election of 1956. But Nixon had influential friends, including Republican National Chairman Leonard Hall, and managed to remain on the ticket. Three families with heavy interests in oil—the Rockefellers, Pews, and Mellons—together gave almost a half million dollars to the Republican forces, led by Ike and Dick.

As was later reported by journalists Drew Pearson and Jack Anderson in *The Case Against Congress*, Eisenhower, who, up to that time, "did more for the nation's private oil and gas interests than any other President," had the upkeep of his Gettysburg farm paid for by three oilmen—Alton W. Jones, the chairman of the executive committee of Cities Service; B. B. Byars of Tyler, Texas; and George E. Allen, a big investor in petroleum.

Businessmen who accepted Cabinet appointments were supposed to "divest" themselves of financial interest in companies to which government contracts might be awarded. But Harold E. Talbott, the president of an airplane company, who became Eisenhower's Secretary of the Air Force, retained a half-interest in a management-engineering firm for which he solicited business while in government service; and Robert T. Ross, who served as an assistant to Ike's Secretary of Defense, Charles E. Wilson, gave millions of dollars' worth of business to a company that was headed by

OILMEN LIKED
REPUBLICANS: The
Rockefellers, Pews, and
Mellons together gave
almost a half million dollars
to help Ike and Dick win
the election of 1956.

his wife. Both men were thrown out of their jobs, and both considered themselves "martyrs"—they had sacrificed so much money to serve their country, what was wrong with their making a little on the side?

Another affair, which rocked the nation with laughter but caused Eisenhower's Secretary of Agriculture Ezra Taft Benson a lot of embarrassment, was the "great cheese scandal." Benson, who was violently opposed to anything that even slightly suggested the existence of a welfare state, dropped the price-support level for all dairy products from 90 to 75 per cent parity on April 1, 1954. Had the Secretary taken the trouble to check things out, he would have undoubtedly discovered that the big cheese distributors of Wisconsin and bordering states had already contracted to sell 90 million pounds of their local "cheddar" to the government at the high-support price of 37 cents a pound. Immediately afterwards, they bought back almost the same amount of

241

cheese from the government at $34\frac{1}{4}$ cents a pound, making a profit of nearly $2.5 million on cheese that had never actually left their warehouses. Much to the surprise of many people, the President did not ask Benson for his resignation.

IKE THE BUCK PASSER

Eisenhower, an amateur in politics, whose conception of the Presidency precluded positive leadership and allowed plenty of time for golf, was, according to most historians, more of a constitutional monarch, a symbolic chief of state, than a dynamic initiator of policy. He mediated and smoothed over difficulties, but left the running of the government to members of his Cabinet and the Republicans in Congress. His Administration was marked by little change in domestic affairs, and, although there was considerable sniping at Franklin D. Roosevelt's New Deal institutions, all basic New Deal measures were continued, and even enlarged upon. Ike meant to balance the federal budget once he was in office, but he found the task too big. Government money continued to pour into foreign aid, American welfare, and grants to farmers. A rising crop of political analysts pictured Ike as being "too lazy to attend to his responsibilities."

EGYPTIAN RELATIONS MISHANDLED

Eisenhower did, indeed, bring peace in Korea, although the huge waste of money and lives gained no ground from the Communists. But after keeping this election promise, he delegated most of the responsibility for foreign affairs to Secretary of State John Foster Dulles, who played a strong hand. The Secretary's policy of firm opposition to Communist expansion, called "brinkmanship," was little more than what President Truman's policy of Communist containment

242

had been. He carried the big "atomic stick" in American air bases encircling Russia; but the stick was never used in a preventive war, although America's stock of nuclear weapons was much larger than Russia's. He did nothing to help the rebels in East Germany in 1953, nothing to help the French in Indochina in 1954, and nothing to help the revolutionists in Hungary in 1956.

The Suez Canal, linking Port Said with the Red Sea, had been built by Compagnie Universelle, a French company, between 1859 and 1869, at a cost of about $87 million, most of which was subscribed to by European governments. The British government, which by 1950 had become the company's largest stockholder, maintained, via a treaty with Egypt, a small military base at Suez. The canal, which had been declared a neutral zone, was to be open to ships of all nations in war as well as in peace. But Egypt's dictator, Gamal Abdel Nasser, did not go along with this idea, and in his implacable hostility to Israel, he denied the canal to her ships. The Security Council of the United Nations ordered Egypt to end this illegal prohibition in 1951, but she refused to comply.

Dulles, all too slow to realize that Nasser was not a "reasonable" dictator like Yugoslavia's Marshal Tito, gave his support to the Egyptian, who forced Great Britain to evacuate her Suez base. It was expected that when this "thorn in Egypt's sovereignty" was removed, Nasser would behave himself.

The Western Powers, knowing that Nasser had to raise some $2 billion to build an immense dam at Aswan for the irrigation of millions of acres of arid land, thought that they would be able to keep him in line by helping him financially. Negotiations between the United States Department of State, Britain's Foreign Office, and the World Bank to foot the initial bill of $70 million, and finance the balance by loans, were completed before the end of 1955. Dulles, however, became increasingly irritated by Nasser's truculence, and by his mortgaging of Egypt's cotton inventory to buy $200 million in guns, planes, and tanks from Russia. Learning of Nasser's dickering with the Russians for a better financial deal for the dam, Dulles, without warning, canceled America's offer to participate in the loan. Great Britain, perforce, followed suit. As historian Samuel Eliot Morison pointed out, this was the worst way to handle an arrogant dictator, who could easily have been kept guessing for many months. Nasser retaliated promptly by seizing the Suez Canal, and grabbing all of the tolls for Egypt's treasury. Sir Anthony Eden, the British prime minister, and Christian Pineau, the French foreign minister, repeatedly pointed out that force would have to be used to recover the canal if Nasser continued to refuse to negotiate. Dulles, who disliked Eden and feared that Britain was out to recover her prewar position in the Middle East, refused to commit himself, but President Eisenhower did so in the worst way, saying "We are committed to a peaceful settlement in this dispute, and nothing else." And that came just at the moment when Sir Robert Menzies, the prime minister of Australia, had persuaded Nasser to negotiate.

Nasser, now assured of Russia's support, felt that he had the Western Powers "over the barrel." But Britain and France, far from being through, took steps to invade the canal zone. Dulles, kept posted on what was going on, knew about this. Israel, suffering from raids by Nasser-supported Arab guerrillas, started hostilities by sending troops into the Sinai peninsula of Egypt on October 29, 1956, giving a sound beating to an Egyptian Army of 45,000, and, in four days, reached the banks of the canal. Eden informed Eisenhower the next day that Britain and France were about to give Israel

244

military support. Dulles was furious, and the President expressed "amazed stupefaction" with the conduct of America's major ally. Nasser quickly blocked the Suez Canal by sinking ships across its channel. The Communist bloc, denouncing the actions of Britain, France, and Israel as "imperialist aggression," threatened to join Egypt unless there was an immediate cease-fire, and hinted at dropping atomic bombs on England and France. It was reasonable to expect that the United States would at least give moral support to the British, French, and Israelis. On the contrary, Eisenhower decided to support *Russian* demands! Britain and France, helpless without America's support, and bumbling in their attempts to occupy Port Said and Suez, announced a cease-fire on November 6, and withdrew their armed forces. Israel threw down her arms early in 1957, after the United States had threatened to stop financial aid, and invoke United Nations sanctions against her.

IKE CAUGHT LYING

The launching of the first Russian "sputnik" caused the United States to worry, and money was poured into research to narrow the "missile gap." There was disaster in Cuba in 1959, when Fidel Castro planted Communism only 90 miles off America's shores.

The disastrous incident of a high-flying American U-2 spy plane, shot down over Russia in the same year, put an end to any hope of improving relations with the Russians. This crisis could not have been handled worse by the White House. First, a routine statement was given out that the plane had simply lost its way when studying the weather, and that no photographic flights deep within Russian territory had been authorized. Then Eisenhower, caught lying, admitted that the Russians were right, and that the plane had been taking photographs to spot Russian nuclear activities. The net result was to put the United States in the wrong, and give Nikita Khrushchev the excuse he needed to stamp the word "aggressor" on the Stars and Stripes.

Francis Cardinal Spellman of New York, hellbent on getting America involved in the Vietnam War to "protect" Vietnamese Catholics, got the President to dispatch some 1,000 "military advisers" to help South Vietnam fight the Communists.

American opinion veered against Eisenhower; the man who had won the "hot war" seemed to be losing the "cold war."

BLACKS GET SOME RIGHTS

The Supreme Court, under Chief Justice Earl Warren, ruled in 1954 that the segregation of black children in public schools was illegal, and that segregation should be brought to an end "with all deliberate speed." All along the border, from Maryland to Missouri, and down to Texas, state and local school authorities undertook— sometimes with more deliberation than speed—to conform to the Court's decision. But a line of bitter resistance ran from Virginia to Louisiana, and eight states, aiming to maintain segregation, passed various laws, most of which were plainly unconstitutional. In 1957, violence broke out in Little Rock, Arkansas, where nine black students tried to enter one of the four public high schools.

Most of the townspeople had expected integration to proceed quietly, and it would have done so, had not Governor Orval E. Faubus, the day before classes started, ordered the National Guard to surround the school, and exclude the black children. Segregationists created a disturbance, and when this blossomed into what looked like an all-out war, President Eisenhower sent in federal troops to restore law and order.

SCHOOLS CLOSED TO BLACKS: Southern public schools, maintaining the idea of segregation, refused to admit blacks to classrooms.

The Little Rock school board appealed to the Supreme Court, which declared: "The constitutional rights [of the children] are not to be sacrificed, or yielded to the violence and disorder which have followed the actions of the Governor. . . . Law and order are not to be preserved by depriving the Negro children of their constitutional rights."

The governor's demagoguery, given worldwide publicity, gave the city, Arkansas, and the whole of America a bad name abroad, and intensified racial antipathies and friction at home; but it also led to a demonstration of supreme federal authority, and showed that segregation was on the way out.

Inspired by the words and activities of the Reverend Martin Luther King, Jr., of Georgia, blacks staged successful demonstrations against segregation in several Southern cities, and, in 1960, began to "sit in" at lunch counters in drug and department stores, where they were allowed to buy goods, but were arrested when they tried to sit down and order a sandwich. Within a short time, the sit-in movement swept the South. The wholesale

247

arrests were all voided by the Supreme Court. Blacks were now ready not only to claim their legal rights, but also to use economic, political, and legal weapons in that struggle. Presently, they would extend their agitation to Northern cities in search of better housing, schools, and status.

It was all very well for Eisenhower to say, "There must be no second-class citizens in this country"—there were, and still are. The traditional American remedy for injustice is political power. The black had lost his right to vote in the reaction against Reconstruction, following the War Between the States. It was now felt that if he regained it, and got elected to at least minor public offices, he could improve his way of life, and force local politicians to respect his wishes.

Accordingly, in 1957, Congress, after 63 days of debate, passed a new civil rights law, the first since 1870, to protect the black's right to vote by removing some of the obstacles that had been imposed by state and local officials. But this law proved to be far too weak to surmount the many tricks that were thought up by dominant Southern whites, or even to overcome the average black's timidity. Eisenhower did complete desegregation in the armed forces, begun under Franklin D. Roosevelt; and in other directions, integration spread. Between 1940 and 1957, the number of black professional men and women more than doubled, the number of skilled workers increased by 181 per cent, and the number of black clerks and salesmen more than tripled.

A CATHOLIC MAKES IT TO THE WHITE HOUSE

America seemed to be afflicted with stagnation in many areas in 1960, and her image was the ailing old general in the White House. Communism had come to the New World, the growth rate of America's economy had begun to sink to half that of Europe, and automation had pushed unemployment to the high level of 4 million. Civil rights measures and legislation to provide medical care for the aged had withered on the vine in Congress for want of leadership from Eisenhower. The Republicans, who had tied their own hands by pushing through the 22nd Amendment to the Constitution limiting a President to two terms, could not pick Ike for a third time around in the election of 1960, so they settled on Richard M. Nixon, who had been "groomed" for the Presidency for eight years. His running mate, Henry Cabot Lodge, II, was a former United States Senator from Massachusetts and Eisenhower's representative to the United Nations.

The Democrats, changing an old "rule" of American politics, picked a Catholic, the 43-year-old Senator John F. Kennedy of Massachusetts, in preference to a Protestant, feeling confident that, if elected President, he would keep his promise not to ask the Pope to move from Rome to Washington, D.C. His running mate, Senator Lyndon B. Johnson of Texas, was chosen for his political power, even though he was reported to have misused his office to expand the Johnson family's radio and television business interests in his native state. He had also been the subject of an article, "Something Is Rotten in the State of Texas," which appeared in a 1951 issue of *Collier's* magazine.

Nixon, aged 47, had no less than four things in common with Kennedy. He, too, was Irish on both sides, and, like Kennedy, he had, as a Congressman and member of the House Un-American Activities Committee, supported Senator McCarthy in his witch hunt for Communists. Also, like Kennedy, Nixon had served in the Navy in World War II, despite his having been brought up as a "peace-loving Quaker"; but when it came to playing poker, Dick did much better than Jack, coming home from the war with a nest egg of around $10,000 that he had won from fellow officers. Both of them were for America's giving aid to the South Vietnamese in their war with the North Vietnamese.

"The prince must be a lion," wrote Machiavelli, "but he must also know how to play the fox." There might be some doubt about Nixon's being a lion, but few would question his being able to play the fox. As journalist Stewart Alsop described him: "He is either the Trick E. Dick of Philip Roth's brutal satire, or the statesman and peace-bringer of the Republican campaign handouts."

Nixon had scarcely entered the final phase of his election campaign against Kennedy when Drew Pearson and Jack Anderson disclosed in their syndicated newspaper column, "Washington Merry-Go-Round," that Dick's brother, Don, had borrowed $205,000 from Howard Hughes, the sequestered multimillionaire, who, at the time of the transaction, was the principal stockholder in Trans World Airlines (T.W.A.). "The loan, secured by a mortgage on . . . a piece of [California] real estate that no bank would have accepted as security for a loan of that size . . . was apparently never repaid," the journalists wrote. "The Hughes Tool Company was an important defense contractor. T.W.A. had applied for an extension of its route from the Philippines to Japan. Hughes himself faced an anti-trust suit. And he had other problems, none of which were likely to become aggravated by the fact that the family of Richard Nixon, a man who might become President of the United States, was beholden to him financially." The press minimized the potential for embarrassment. In New England, where 43 newspapers normally ran "Washington Merry-Go-Round," only three carried the column. Shortly afterwards, the officers and directors of the American

Petroleum Institute forked over $113,000 to Dick's campaign chest, but gave only $6,000 to Jack's.

Judging from what journalist Arthur Krock wrote in *The Consent of the Governed and Other Deceits*, Lyndon B. Johnson, who had been a protégé of Franklin D. Roosevelt, did not like the idea of being "Number Two" man in the election of 1960, but Kennedy and his people made him "acutely aware that he was," and forever reminded him that it was J.F.K. who had won the nomination for the Presidency, not L.B.J. Though Kennedy gave Johnson important assignments throughout the campaign, there was always "an atmosphere of contrivance in the action." The inner Kennedy circle "ridiculed Johnson," and he heard of it, heard of their "exaggerated imitation of his Southwest country accent," and knew they accounted him a "vulgar person." Kennedy once remarked, "I wish I could find something to keep Lyndon happy." But Kennedy never did—nor could.

As Krock pointed out, if Kennedy had not had Johnson, and had not been so much more photogenic on television than Nixon, "he would have been defeated. . . ."

Everyone knows what happened after 1960.

NOTES AND SOURCES

1. The Early Explorers

The allegation that Christopher Columbus and five of the seamen who manned his ships, and four of the principal supporters of his "great adventure" were Jewish is also contained in *Jews, Justice and Judaism*, by Robert St. John (New York: Doubleday & Company, Inc., 1969), and further covered in *Sails of Hope: The Secret Mission of Christopher Columbus*, by Simon Wiesenthal (New York: The Macmillan Company, 1973). The quotation from Columbus's diary, referring to the expulsion of Jews from Spain, similarly appears in St. John, *op. cit.*

The contention that the American Indians were descendants of the ancient Israelites, credited to the Reverend Thomas Thorowgood's *Jews in America, or Probabilities That the Americans Are of that Race* (circa 1642), is also found in St. John, *ibid.*

The excerpt from Martin Waldseemuller's *Cosmographiae Introductio*, pertinent to the naming of America, and the statement made by Columbus, pertinent to an "Other World," are also found in *The Oxford History of the American People*, by Samuel Eliot Morison (New York: Oxford University Press, 1965).

Resource material for the Spanish, Dutch, French, and English explorers, and the American Indians comes from Morison, *op. cit.*; *The Historian's History of the United States*, edited by Andrew S. Berky and James F. Shenton (New York: G.P. Putnam's Sons, 1966); and *A Concise History of the United States*, by Andrew Sinclair (New York: The Viking Press, 1967).

The legend of Pocahontas and the quotation from her husband, John Rolfe, are also contained in Sinclair, *op. cit.*

2. Impure Puritans

Historical narrative and quotations in this chapter are also found in Morison, *op. cit.*; Berky and Shenton, *op. cit.*; and *The Indian and the White Man*, edited by Wilcomb E. Washburn (New York: Anchor Books, Doubleday & Company, Inc., 1964).

The material covering the Reverend Cotton Mather and witchcraft, King Philip's War, slavery, and smuggling also appears in Morison, *ibid.*; Washburn, *op. cit.*; and *No More Lies: The Myth and the Reality of American History*, by Richard Claxton Gregory (New York: Harper & Row, 1971).

The quotation from Gertrude Stein, describing the "purity" of the Puritans, as well as the reference to the behavior of Harvard students, is also found in Morison, *ibid.*

3. Blacks Without Rights

The principal sources for the material concerning slavery, miscegenation, and the names of prominent Americans who used slaves were: *The Afro-American in United States History*, by Benjamin DaSilva, Milton Finkelstein, Arlene Loshin, and Jawn A. Sandifer (New York: Globe Book Company, 1969); *A Documentary History of the Negro People in the United States*, edited by Herbert Aptheker, with a Preface by Dr. W. E. B. Dubois (New York: The Citadel Press, 1969); *Slave Ships and Slaving*, by George Francis Dow (New York: Dover Publications, Inc., 1970); and *White Over Black*, by Winthrop D. Jordan (Chapel Hill, North Carolina: The University of North Carolina Press, 1968).

The story of Thomas Jefferson's affair with Sally Hemings, credited to James T. Callendar in the *Richmond Recorder*, and the quotations from Benjamin Franklin and William Byrd, pertinent to blacks in America, are also found in Jordan, *op. cit.*

4. France in America

Historical narrative and quotations contained in this chapter are also found in *The Growth of the American Republic*, by Samuel Eliot Morison and Henry Steele Commager (New York: Oxford University Press, 1962); Morison, *op. cit.*; and Sinclair, *op. cit.*

5. Rebellion in Virginia

Background material for the poor whites and the Susquehannock Indians, Colonel John Washington, Major John Truman, Governor William Berkeley, and Nathaniel Bacon comes from Berky and Shenton, *op. cit.*; Washburn, *op. cit.*; Morison, *op. cit.*; *The Landmark History of the American People*, by Daniel J. Boorstin (New York: Random House, 1968); and *A Short History of the United States*, by Allan Nevins and Henry Steele Commager (New York: The Modern Library, 1969).

The quotations from Bacon and Berkeley are also contained in Morison, *ibid.*, and Nevins and Commager, *op. cit.*

6. Piracy in the West Indies

Sources for the material concerning the West Indies were: Morison, *op. cit.*; Jordan, *op. cit.*; Morison and Commager, *op. cit.*; and Dow, *op. cit.*

The quotation, pertinent to Barbados rum, is also found in Morison, *ibid.*; and the description of the white men of the island, credited to Bryan Edward's *History of the British West Indies*, is also found in Jordan, *ibid.* The story of the rebellion in Saint-Domingue (Haiti), led by Toussaint L'Ouverture, similarly appears in Jordan, *ibid.*

7. Stubborn New England

Historical narrative and quotations contained in this chapter are also found in Morison, *op. cit.*; Berky and Shenton, *op. cit.*; Morison and Commager, *op. cit.*; and Nevins and Commager, *op. cit.*

The story of the New Englanders and their "gift package" for King Charles II and the story of the New Yorkers and their hanging of Jacob Leisler also appear in Morison, *ibid.*

8. Penn's Holy Experiment

The reference to Thomas E. Drake's *Quakers and Slavery* is also found in Jordan, *op. cit.*

The description of how the Penn family tricked the Conestoga Indians also appears in Morison, *op. cit.*

The remark about the Quakers and the way they treated their neighbors, credited to John Blackwell, is similarly contained in Morison, *ibid.*

Background material for Penn and the Quakers, in general, comes from Berky and Shenton, *op. cit.*

9. The Jews' Troubles

Historical narrative and quotations contained in this chapter are also found in St. John, *op. cit.*; and *Early American Jewry*, by Jacob Rader Marcus (Philadelphia: The Jewish Publication Society of America, 5721–1961).

10. Revolutionary Schemers

Resource material for the 13 American colonies comes from Berky and Shenton, *op. cit.*; Boorstin, *op. cit.*; Morison, *op. cit.*; John C. Miller's essay, "Origins of the American Revolution," in Berky and Shenton, *ibid.*; and *Pioneers and Patriots*, by Lavinia Dobler and Edgar A. Toppin (New York: Doubleday and Company, Inc., 1965).

The descriptions of the real estate dealings of George Washington and Benjamin Franklin are also found in Morison, *ibid.*

The quotations from John Adams, Benjamin Franklin, and Samuel Adams, concerning the "Boston Massacre," Britain's lowering of taxes, and the "Boston Tea Party," are also contained in Morison, *ibid.*, and Nevins and Commager, *op. cit.*

11. Independence Declared

Sources for the material contained in this chapter were: *In Quest of Freedom: American Political Thought and Practice*, by A. Thomas Mason and R. H. Leach (Englewood Cliffs, New Jersey: Prentice-Hall, Inc., 1959); and *Our Republic*, by Joseph Aubrey (Utica, New York: T. J. Griffiths, 1891).

The quotations, credited to David Cooper, also appear in Jordan, *op. cit.*

The quotations, credited to Oliver Wendell Holmes, also appear in Aubrey, *op. cit.*

The quotations, credited to Washington, Hamilton, Jay, and Adams, are similarly contained in Mason and Leach, *op. cit.*

12. The Patriots

The story of the way George Washington collected for his services as commander-in-chief of the Continental Army, together with the story of the love affair he reportedly carried on with Mary Gibbons, is also told in *George Washington's Expense Account*, by George Washington and Marvin Kitman (New York: Simon and Schuster, 1970).

The story of the possibility that Franklin "may indeed have been an enemy agent" is covered at length in *Code Number 72/Benjamin Franklin: Patriot or Spy?* by Cecil B. Currey (Englewood Cliffs, New Jersey: Prentice-Hall, Inc., 1972).

The story of Mrs. Robert Murray and British General William Howe is also contained in *The Compact History of the Revolutionary War*, by Colonel R. Ernest Dupuy and Colonel Trevor N. Dupuy (New York: Hawthorn Books, Inc., 1963).

Background material for the American Revolution comes from Morison, *op. cit.*; Dupuy and Dupuy, *op. cit.*; *From Colony to World Power: A History of the United States*, by William A. Hamm (Boston: D.C. Heath and Company, 1947); *Those Damned Rebels: The American Revolution As Seen Through British Eyes*, by Michael Pearson (New York: G.P. Putnam's Sons, 1972); and Currey, *op. cit.*

13. A Government Is Constituted

Resource material for this chapter is found in Sinclair, *op. cit.*; *The Consent of the Governed and Other Deceits*, by Arthur Krock (Boston-Toronto: Little, Brown and Company, 1971); *Time* magazine (see below); *Government of the People*, by Senator Kenneth B. Keating (Cleveland-New York: The World Publishing Company, 1964); *Government by the People*, by James MacGregor

256

Burns and Jack Walter Peltason (Englewood Cliffs, New Jersey: Prentice-Hall, Inc., 1952); and *Congress: The Sapless Branch*, by Joseph S. Clark (New York: Harper & Row, Publishers, 1965).

The quotation from Alexis de Tocqueville, pertinent to America's love of money, is from his book *Democracy in America*, edited by Richard D. Heffner (New York and Scarborough, Ontario: New American Library, 1956).

The quotations from Harry S. Truman and Thomas R. Marshall, pertinent to America's Vice Presidents, are also found in a *Time* magazine essay, "There Must Be a Better Way to Choose," August 7, 1972; the quotation from Charles Jones, pertinent to Congress, is also found in a *Time* magazine cover story, "The Crack in the Constitution," January 15, 1973.

The quotation from Roscoe Drummond's column in the *Washington Post*, pertinent to the election of 1960, also appears in Keating, *op. cit.*

14. Washington as President

Historical narrative and quotations contained in this chapter are also contained in Morison, *op. cit.*; Mason and Leach, *op. cit.*; and Sinclair, *op. cit.*

The quotation from the *Philadelphia Aurora*, pertinent to Washington's retirement, is also found in Morison, *ibid.*

15. Adams Versus Jefferson

Sources for the material concerning Adams, Jefferson, Burr, Hamilton, Jackson, Marshall, and Astor were: Hamm, *op. cit.*; Morison, *op. cit.*; Nevins and Commager, *op. cit.*; St. John, *op. cit.*; *Time* magazine (see below); and Jordan, *op. cit.*

The fact that Adams played "hookey" as President, as well as the fact that he violated the Constitution while in office, also appears in Morison, *ibid.*

The report that both Maryland and New Hampshire maintained a religious ban against Jews holding public office is also found in St. John, *ibid.*

The story of "General" Gabriel's rebellion is also contained in Jordan, *ibid.*

The quotation from Chief Justice Marshall, pertinent to President Jefferson's being subpoenaed in the trial of Aaron Burr, also appears in a *Time* magazine cover story, "Battle Over Presidential Power," August 6, 1973.

The story of the "tricky" Mr. Astor is also found in Morison, *ibid.*

16. The Second War with England

Historical narrative and quotations in this chapter are also found in Sinclair, *op. cit.*; Morison, *op. cit.*; and St. John, *op. cit.*

The story of Uriah Phillips Levy and the embarrassment he suffered as a Jew in the Navy also appears in St. John, *ibid.*

The quotation from Washington Irving, describing Madison, is also contained in Sinclair, *ibid.*; the quotation from Senator Benton, pertinent to "money power," is also contained in Morison, *ibid.*

17. Elections by Foul Means

Background material for the elections of 1824 and 1828, as well as for Jackson's Administration and his "brand" of democracy, comes from Sinclair, *op. cit.*; Morison, *op. cit.*; and *Facts About the Presidents from Washington to Johnson*, by Joseph Nathan Kane (New York: Pocket Books, 1968).

The quotation from the Bible, credited to the pastor of the capital's Unitarian church at this time, is also found in Morison, *ibid.*

The story of Senator Eaton's love affair with Peggy O'Neale similarly appears in Morison, *ibid.*

The quotation, credited to John Quincy Adams in reference to Harvard's conferring an honorary degree on Jackson, is also contained in Kane, *op. cit.*

18. Extending Freedom (and Slavery)

Historical narrative and quotations contained in this chapter, including James Russell Lowell's poem from his *Biglow Papers*, are also found in Morison, *op. cit.*; and Morison and Commager, *op. cit.*

19. A Bit of Horse Trading

Sources for the material concerning the Kansas-Nebraska Act, along with quotations and other material contained in this chapter, were: Berky and Shenton, *op. cit.*; Sinclair, *op. cit.*; and Morison, *op. cit.*

The stories of the Know-Nothings and the "Young Americans," as well as those about Daniel Webster, Louis Kossuth, Solon Borland, Cornelius Vanderbilt, and William Walker, are also found in Morison, *ibid.*

20. On the Road to War

Historical narrative and quotations, contained in this chapter, are also found in *Minorities: U.S.A.*, by Milton Finkelstein, Jawn A. Sandifer, and Elfreda S. Wright (New York: Globe Book

Company, 1971); Burns and Peltason, *op. cit.*; and Morison, *op. cit.*
The story of Senators Sumner and Butler, and Congressman Brooks, as well as the quotations credited to Ralph Waldo Emerson, the *Richmond Enquirer*, and William Cullen Bryant similarly appears in Morison, *ibid.*

21. A Nation Under Two Flags
Sources for the material contained in this chapter were: *The Second Rebellion*, by James McCague (New York: The Dial Press, Inc., 1968); Berky and Shenton, *op. cit.*; Morison, *op. cit.*; *Look Out Whitey! Black Power's Gon' Get Your Mama*, by Julius Lester (New York: The Dial Press, Inc., 1968); Sinclair, *op. cit.*; and *The Robber Barons*, by Matthew Josephson (New York: Harcourt, Brace & World, Inc., 1962).
The quotation from Archbishop Hughes, pertinent to Catholics being unwilling to fight for the abolition of slavery, is also found in Morison, *ibid.*
The story about P. T. Barnum's circus, credited to the *New York Times*, similarly appears in Morison, *ibid.*
The stories about John D. Rockefeller, Philip D. Armour, Cornelius Vanderbilt, James Mellon, Jay Cooke, Salmon P. Chase, Simon Stevens, and J. P. Morgan are also contained in Josephson, *op. cit.* The reference to Vanderbilt's "splitting" commissions with his agent, similarly appears in Josephson, *ibid.*
The quotation from the editor of the *Richmond Examiner*, quoting eggs at one dollar each, is also found in Morison, *ibid.*

22. Impeachment and Reconstruction
Resource material for this chapter is found in Berky and Shenton, *op. cit.*; Morison, *op. cit.*; Nevins and Commager, *op. cit.*; and Sinclair, *op. cit.*
The story of the Irish Revolutionary Brotherhood's invasion of Canada also appears in Morison, *ibid.*

23. Grant's "Gilded Age"
Historical narrative and quotations contained in this chapter are also found in Josephson, *op. cit.*; Hamm, *op. cit.*; Morison, *op. cit.*; the *New York Sunday News* (see below); and *Time* magazine (see below).
The quotation from Senator Grimes, describing the Republican party, is also contained in Morison, *ibid.*
The stories about Jay Gould and Jim Fisk, "Boss" Tweed, the

Supreme Court, Department of the Interior, Treasury Department, Navy yards, Commander Mahan, Congressman Butler, and General Belknap also appear in Josephson, *ibid.*

The quotation from Henry Adams, concerning the scandals of the day, is also found in Morison, *ibid.*

The story about the St. Louis "Whisky Ring," as well as the story about the crookedness of Thomas Murphy, similarly appears in a *New York Sunday News* feature story, "Latest in a Long Line of White House Scandals," May 6, 1973.

The story about Thomas C. Durant and Congressman Ames, in connection with the Credit Mobilier scandal, is also found in Josephson, *ibid.*

The story of Vice President Schuyler Colfax and the charges leveled against him, similarly appears in a *Time* magazine story, "Impeaching a Veep: The Colfax Case," October 1, 1973.

The story of Senator Conkling, Congressman Garfield, and Senator Blaine and the way they bought stock in corporations is also found in Hamm, *ibid.*

The poem, written by James Russell Lowell to celebrate America's 100th birthday, also appears in Morison, *ibid.*

24. Corruption Extended

Sources for the material contained in this chapter were: Sinclair, *op. cit.*; Nevins and Commager, *op. cit.*; Berky and Shenton, *op. cit.*; Morison, *op. cit.*; Josephson, *op. cit.*; and *The Negro and the American Labor Movement*, edited by Julius Jacobson (New York: Doubleday & Company, Inc., Anchor Books, 1968).

The quotation from James Bryce, pertinent to corrupt city bosses, is also found in Sinclair, *ibid.*

The material concerning Armour, American Sugar Refining, Michigan Salt Trust, Standard Oil, American Tobacco, Carnegie Steel, and United States Steel is also found in Nevins and Commager, *ibid.*; and Josephson, *ibid.*

The material concerning the New York Central, Union Pacific, Great Northern, Central Pacific, and Southern Pacific Railroads is also contained in Morison, *ibid.*, and Josephson, *ibid.*

The material concerning the Baltimore & Ohio and Pennsylvania Railroads in the "Great Strike of '77," as well as the material concerning the strikes at McCormick Harvester Machine Company, Carnegie Steel, and the Pullman Company, is also found in Nevins and Commager, *ibid.*, and Josephson, *ibid.* The quotation from

President Cleveland, pertinent to the Pullman strike, similarly appears in Josephson, *ibid.*

The material concerning the American Federation of Labor and its refusal to do anything to help black wage earners is also contained in Morison, *ibid.*

25. The "Gay" Nineties

Historical narrative and quotations contained in this chapter are also found in Josephson, *op. cit.*; Berky and Shenton, *op. cit.*; Finkelstein, Sandifer, and Wright, *op. cit.*; St. John, *op. cit.*; and Sinclair, *op. cit.*

The quotation from Henry Adams, describing the wealthy as unfit parents, also appears in Josephson, *ibid.*

The material concerning anti-Semitism in America, as well as the material concerning the anti-Semitic actions and remarks of Henry Hilton and Austin Corbin, is also contained in St. John, *ibid.*

The quotation from the Reverend Beecher is similarly found in St. John, *ibid.*

The quotation from Senator Beveridge is also found in Sinclair, *ibid.*

26. Teddy the Trust Buster

Background sources for this chapter were: Sinclair, *op. cit.*; Morison, *op. cit.*; Josephson, *op. cit.*; and Hamm, *op. cit.*

The quotation from Mark Twain, pertinent to Theodore Roosevelt, is also found in Sinclair, *ibid.*

The material concerning Senators Platt, Hanna, and LaFollette, and President Taft also appears in Hamm, *ibid.*

The material concerning the strike at the Philadelphia & Reading Coal & Iron Company, as well as the material concerning J. P. Morgan, the Vanderbilts, A. J. Cassatt, G. F. Baer, and John Mitchell, is also contained in Josephson, *ibid.*

The reference to *The Jungle*, by Upton Sinclair, also appears in Morison, *ibid.*

The material concerning the Northern Securities Company and its organizers—Morgan, Harriman, and Hill—is also found in Josephson, *ibid.*

27. Professor at the Helm

Historical narrative and quotations, contained in this chapter, are also found in Berky and Shenton, *op. cit.*; Sinclair, *op. cit.*;

Morison, *op. cit.*; Burns and Peltason, *op. cit.*; St. John, *op. cit.*; and Finkelstein, Sandifer, and Wright, *op. cit.*

The material concerning the hanging of Leo M. Frank, as well as the quotations from *The Jeffersonian* and the *Marietta Journal*, is also found in Finkelstein, Sandifer, and Wright, *ibid.*

The quotation from President Wilson, pertinent to America's neutrality in 1914, also appears in Sinclair, *ibid.*

The material concerning the Espionage and Sedition Acts is also contained in Burns and Peltason, *ibid.*

The material concerning Attorney General Palmer's crackdown on "Reds," as well as the material concerning Henry Ford's anti-Semitic activities, is also found in St. John, *ibid.*, and Morison, *ibid.*

28. Harding and the "Ohio Gang"

Sources for the material contained in this chapter were: *In the Time of Silent Cal: A Retrospective History of the 1920's*, by Jules Abels (New York: G.P. Putnam's Sons, 1969); Morison, *op. cit.*; Gregory, *op. cit.*; Hamm, *op. cit.*; and the *New York Sunday News* (see below).

The quotation from Walter Lippmann, diagnosing Harding's election, is also found in Morison, *ibid.*

The quotation from Frank Waterman Stearns, pertinent to Coolidge, also appears in Abels, *ibid.*

The quotation from T. S. Eliot, describing Harding's appointees as "hollow men," is also found in Morison, *ibid.*

The story of Nan Britton, her book, *The President's Daughter*, and how she served as Harding's mistress, similarly appears in a *New York Sunday News* feature story, "Latest in a Long Line of White House Scandals," May 6, 1973.

The material concerning Teapot Dome, as well as the reference to the *St. Louis Post–Dispatch*, is also found in Morison, *ibid.*, and Hamm, *ibid.*

The quotation from the Reverend Henry van Dyke of New York City's Brick Presbyterian Church, pertinent to Jazz, also appears in Morison, *ibid.*

The story of Sacco-Vanzetti is also found in Abels, *ibid.*, and Gregory, *ibid.*

The material concerning Kenneth Roberts and his articles in the *Saturday Evening Post*, pertinent to immigration, also appears in Morison, *ibid.*

29. "Silent Cal"

Background sources for this chapter were: Abels, *op. cit.*; Morison, *op. cit.*; and Sinclair, *op. cit.*

The quotations from Frank R. Kent, H.L. Mencken, Calvin Coolidge, Lincoln Steffens, National Association of Manufacturers, and Heywood Broun, as well as the references to Andrew W. Mellon, William E. Humphrey, and William Culbertson, are also found in Abels, *ibid.*

The story of Aaron Sapiro and Henry Ford similarly appears in Abels, *ibid.*

The material concerning William Phillips and Canada is also found in Morison, *ibid.*

30. The Great Depression

Sources for the material contained in this chapter were: Burns and Peltason, *op. cit.*; Sinclair, *op. cit.*; Morison, *op. cit.*; *The Plot to Seize the White House*, by Jules Archer (New York: Hawthorn Books, Inc., 1973); and *The Money Lords*, by Matthew Josephson (New York: Weybright and Talley, 1972).

The story of the way Army and Navy veterans were roughed up on President Hoover's orders, and driven away from the White House by armed troops, led by MacArthur and Eisenhower, similarly appears in Archer, *op. cit.*; and Sinclair, *ibid.*

The quotations from the National Association of Manufacturers, John D. Rockefeller, and Andrew W. Mellon, as well as the stories of Samuel E. Insull, Ivar Kreuger, James V. Forrestal, and the United States & Foreign Securities Corporation, are also found in Morison, *ibid.*; and Josephson, *op. cit.*

31. F.D.R.'s New Deal

Historical narrative and quotations contained in this chapter are also found in Sinclair, *op. cit.*; Gregory, *op. cit.*; Morison, *op. cit.*; Archer, *op. cit.*; *The Case Against Congress*, by Drew Pearson and Jack Anderson (New York: Simon and Schuster, 1968); Krock, *op. cit.*; and *An Untold Story: The Roosevelts of Hyde Park*, by Elliott Roosevelt and James Brough (New York: G. P. Putnam's Sons, 1973).

The quotation from Will Rogers, pertinent to the election of 1932, also appears in Morison, *ibid.*

The material concerning wages in the Great Depression is also contained in Gregory, *ibid.*

The quotation from the *New York Times*, pertinent to the decline in lynchings in the United States, is similarly found in Gregory, *ibid.*

Material concerning Pelley, Dennis, Smith, Coughlin, Hearst, Pound, Kaltenbach, Goldsborough, Browder, Hiss, and Chambers also appears in Morison, *ibid.*

The story of the National Maritime Union and the way it threatened national defense is also found in Morison, *ibid.*

The story of the American Liberty League and its attempt to take over the government of the United States is told at length in Archer, *ibid.*

The account of the Catholic lobby, including the censorship of magazines and the advocacy of the embargo against arms to European nations, is also found in Pearson and Anderson, *op. cit.* The account of R.C.A. and its deals with other corporations, together with the account of its involvement in an anti-trust suit, similarly appears in Pearson and Anderson, *ibid.*

The story of Japanese-Americans and the way they were forced to live in concentration camps in World War II, as well as the quotation from Morton Grodzin's *Americans Betrayed*, is also found in Gregory, *ibid.*

The story of Eleanor Roosevelt's "unhappy days" with F.D.R. is told at length in Roosevelt and Brough, *op. cit.*

32. The Truman Scandals

Resource material for this chapter comes from Sinclair, *op. cit.*; Morison, *op. cit.*; *The Truman Scandals*, by Jules Abels (Chicago: Henry Regnery Company, 1956); Finkelstein, Sandifer, and Wright, *op. cit.*; the *New York Times* (see below); *Life* magazine (see below); Gregory, *op. cit.*; and the *Facts File of the New York Public Library (National Affairs/Labor—May 1, 1952).*

The stories of Truman's cronies also appear in Abels, *op. cit.*, and Morison, *ibid.*

The story concerning the members of the Al Capone gang and the way they were paroled similarly appears in Abels, *ibid.*

The letter, written by the Hopi Indians to Truman, protesting the grabbing of their lands by oilmen, is also found in Finkelstein, Sandifer, and Wright, *ibid.*

The contention of the N.A.A.C.P. that blacks were denied membership in labor unions also appears in Gregory, *ibid.*

The story of the "secret oil deal" in the Middle East in 1950 is also found in a *New York Times* front-page story, "Oil Profits, Treasury Losses Linked to Secret Decision," January 31, 1974.

The story of Truman's seizure of the steel mills in 1952 is similarly reported in *Life* magazine, April 12, 1952, under "Truman and Steel."

33. "Ike" and "Dick"

Historical narrative and quotations contained in this chapter are also found in Morison, *op. cit.*; Sinclair, *op. cit.*; Nevins and Commager, *op. cit.*; Pearson and Anderson, *op. cit.*; Krock, *op. cit.*; *America, Inc.: Who Owns and Operates the United States*, by Morton Mintz and Jerry S. Cohen (New York: The Dial Press, 1971); *The Atlantic* magazine (see below); *Plain Speaking*, by Merle Miller (New York: G. P. Putnam's Sons, 1974); *The Strange Case of Richard Milhous Nixon*, by Jerry Voorhis (New York: Popular Library, 1973); and *Perfectly Clear: Nixon from Whittier to Watergate*, by Frank Mankiewicz (New York: Quadrangle/The New York Times Book Co., 1973).

The *New York Post* account of Nixon's "secret fund," as well as the reference to his "Checkers" speech, also appears in Mankiewicz, *op. cit.*, and Mintz and Cohen, *op. cit.*

The story of the McCarthy witch hunt for Reds is also contained in Morison, *ibid.*

The quotations from Harry S. Truman, pertinent to Eisenhower and Nixon, are also found in Miller, *op. cit.*

The story of Eisenhower's "deputy President," Sherman Adams, and the members of the President's Cabinet, including Dulles, Anderson, Talbott, Ross, and Benson, also appears in Morison, *ibid.*

Material included under the subheadings of "Egyptian Relations Mishandled" and "Ike Caught Lying" is similarly found in Morison, *ibid.*

Material included under the subheading of "Blacks Get Some Rights" is also contained in Nevins and Commager, *ibid.*

The reference to Nixon's poker playing, and to his winning $10,000 from fellow officers in the Navy in World War II, is also incorporated in a magazine article, "Nixon and the Square Majority," by Stewart Alsop, which appears in the February, 1972, issue of *The Atlantic*.

INDEX

271